# More Praise for *Getting to Resolution*

"*Getting to Resolution* offers a unique and effective paradigm for understanding how you can use your natural gifts and interconnectedness to improve your interactions in all relationships."

Marvin E. Johnson, JD, Executive Director,
Center for Alternative Dispute Resolution

"*Getting to Resolution* is a clear and practical guide to the secret of success — how to create and leverage collaborative advantage. It is a must read for leaders seeking to strengthen relationships and get positive results."

Diana Whitney, PhD, President, Corporation for Positive Change,
and coauthor of *The Power of Appreciative Inquiry*, *The Appreciative Inquiry Summit*, and *Appreciative Inquiry: A Positive Revolution in Change*

"It is impossible to read this book and not grow in understanding of conflict, resolution, and self. Every page offers wisdom and practical tools."

Arnie Herz, Esq.

"Stewart Levine has written a very practical book about one of life's vexing problems — how to reach agreement with others when differences must be resolved. He does so with the intent of fostering collaboration and creativity as the outcome."

Alan Briskin, author of *The Stirring of Soul in the Workplace*
and coauthor of *The Power of Collective Wisdom*

"This book is practical, mind-altering, and life-changing. It's hard to achieve those in one book, but *Getting to Resolution* does that. It fills you with inner peace and the wisdom to untangle the thorniest conflict."

Noah Blumenthal, author of the
*Wall Street Journal* bestseller *Be the Hero*

"If you want to resolve conflict and build relationships while connecting at a profound level, read *Getting to Resolution*. It gives you new language and practices for transforming your communication so you can lead at a higher level."

Victoria Halsey, PhD, Vice President of Applied Learning,
The Ken Blanchard Companies, and coauthor of
*The Hamster Revolution* and *The Hamster Revolution for Meetings*

# Praise for the **First Edition**

"He has developed techniques to resolve conflict and maximize satisfaction among all parties involved...Levine's approach is refreshingly practical."

*Booklist*

"His plan will go a long way to reducing the stress involved in collaborating with others and achieving a resolution which all parties find acceptable. A must read."

*Law Practice Management*

"His process has real application...He makes the process accessible... Recommended for all public libraries."

*Library Journal*

"Stewart Levine succeeds in changing our thinking about conflict, providing a model for resolution, and enabling us to take personal responsibility for dealing with conflict and diversity."

*The School Administrator*

"Promotes a new way of thinking that shifts our focus from rights and entitlements to service and responsibility."

*Financial Sentinel*

"Tools that get to the core of every conflict."

*Dayton News*

"The book reveals real wisdom."

*Family Advocate*

"*Getting to Resolution* offers a road map to finding common ground with reduced acrimony. Levine might have called it 'Getting to Relationship.'"

Lawrence Richard, JD, PhD

"The model goes to the heart of our relationship with ourselves and others and injects a conscious awareness that brings us to a level of personal responsibility from which we can expand our lives."

David Rotman, Esq., Mediator, Gregorio, Haldeman & Piazza

"Levine's experiences give him the ability to see our culture more broadly. I applaud his work on driving us to understand the benefits of agreement and away from conflict."

Lance R. Primis, former President and COO,
The New York Times Company

"Ultimately practical, it allows you to experience the relief and satisfaction of 'win-win' relationships."

Michael Lanier, former CIO, Charles Schwab and DHL

"Value for everyone who seeks to function effectively in society. *Getting to Resolution* will make it easier to use energy productively that would otherwise be wasted in confrontation."

Richard W. Odgers, Esq., Senior Partner, Pillsbury Winthrop, and former General Counsel, Pacific Telesis

"The book will teach you how to get the best each individual has to offer by providing a behavioral model that promotes individual contribution to problem solving."

Steven J. Noble, PhD, former Executive Director, Human Resources Planning Society

"The power of collaboration is illuminated by real stories about real people. The book shows the importance of learning to listen and that agreement is the joyous outcome of a process of discovery and mutual commitment."

Nina B. Link, President and CEO, Magazine Publishers of America

"An important tool for the hectic time we live in. A reminder that civilization rests on our ability to communicate with each other."

Lord Graham of Edmonton, former Chief Whip, House of Lords

## Praise for *The Book of Agreement*

"With less focus on the purely psychological aspects of reaching agreement than *Getting to Yes*, Levine's book becomes a much more pragmatic approach."

*Perdido*

"Among the best of 2003."

*The CEO Refresher*

"It was like a whack on the side of the head when I embraced Levine's notion that we'd all benefit from embracing the idea of creating agreements for results instead of negotiating agreements for protection. The pages are full of explicit advice on how to do it."

James M. Kouzes, coauthor of *The Leadership Challenge* and *Encouraging the Heart*

"We all want agreement. Here's how to get it and keep it and work it."
Mark Victor Hansen, cocreator, #1 *New York Times*
bestselling series Chicken Soup for the Soul

"*The Book of Agreement* contains all the models you'll ever need to protect questionable relationships and nurture strong relationships. It puts some iron in the handshake."
Alan Weiss, PhD, author of *The Ultimate Consultant*

"Lawyers learn to reproduce mistrust by learning that the purpose of legal agreements is to protect you from the Other who is out to exploit you. Levine begins from the opposite premise — that the purpose of agreement is to build a bridge to the Other and realize your common aspiration for connection. This idea could help realize our spiritual nature as social beings in pursuit of mutual affirmation."
Peter Gabel, Professor of Contract Law; Associate Editor, *Tikkun*;
and President of the Board, New College of California

"Stewart explains the art and the science of this elusive word. Readers will quickly be able to apply his ideas, suggestions, and experience. He maps the confusing and difficult territory of agreement so all of us can make this difficult process easier."
Beverly Kaye, coauthor of *Love 'Em or Lose 'Em;* author of *Up Is Not the Only Way;* and founder and President, Career Systems International

"Buy this book. I know systems for creating wealth. The system will help you create the kind of agreements that will generate more financial and emotional wealth in your life."
Robert Allen, author of the four *New York Times*
bestsellers *Creating Wealth, Multiple Streams of Income, Multiple Streams of Internet Income,* and *Nothing Down*

"Stewart makes it clear our standard approaches to building agreements must change. He provides the philosophical and practical tools for individuals and institutions to transform their approaches and build a better world."
Steven Keeva, former Assistant Managing Editor,
*American Bar Association Journal,* and author of *Transforming Practices*

# Get-
# ting
# to
# reso-
# lu-
# tion

# Get-ting to reso-lu-tion

**Second Edition**

**Stewart Levine**

## TURNING CONFLICT INTO COLLABORATION

BK

Berrett–Koehler Publishers, Inc.
San Francisco
*a BK Business book*

Berrett-Koehler Publishers, Inc.
235 Montgomery Street, Suite 650
San Francisco, CA 94104-2916
Tel: (415) 288-0260    Fax: (415) 362-2512    www.bkconnection.com

**Ordering Information**
**Quantity sales.** Special discounts are available on quantity purchases by corporations, associations, and others. For details, contact the "Special Sales Department" at the Berrett-Koehler address above.
**Individual sales.** Berrett-Koehler publications are available through most bookstores. They can also be ordered directly from Berrett-Koehler:
Tel: (800) 929-2929; Fax: (802) 864-7626; www.bkconnection.com
**Orders for college textbook/course adoption use.** Please contact Berrett-Koehler:
Tel: (800) 929-2929; Fax: (802) 864-7626.
**Orders by U.S. trade bookstores and wholesalers.** Please contact Ingram Publisher Services, Tel: (800) 509-4887; Fax: (800) 838-1149;
E-mail: customer.service@ingrampublisherservices.com; or visit www.ingrampublisherservices.com/Ordering for details about electronic ordering.

Berrett-Koehler and the BK logo are registered trademarks of Berrett-Koehler Publishers, Inc.

Printed in the United States of America

Berrett-Koehler books are printed on long-lasting acid-free paper. When it is available, we choose paper that has been manufactured by environmentally responsible processes. These may include using trees grown in sustainable forests, incorporating recycled paper, minimizing chlorine in bleaching, or recycling the energy produced at the paper mill.

*Library of Congress Cataloging-in-Publication Data*
Levine, Stewart.
   Getting to resolution : turning conflict into collaboration / Stewart Levine. —2nd ed.
      p. cm.
   Includes bibliographical references and index.
   ISBN 978-1-57675-771-0 (pbk. : alk. paper)
   1. Dispute resolution (Law)—United States. 2. Mediation—United States. 3. Conflict management. I. Title.
   KF9084.L48 2009
   347.73'9—dc22

                                                                2009028809

Second Edition
15 14 13 12 11 10 09            10 9 8 7 6 5 4 3 2 1

Text designer, Detta Penna; copyeditor, Judith Johnstone; proofreader, Susan Padgett; indexer, Joan Dickey

*For Martha, with gratitude*

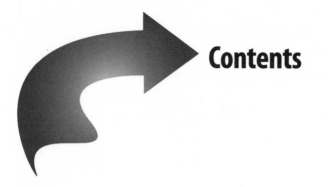

# Contents

**Resource D**

# The Cycle of Resolution 248

If you knew the secret history of those you would like to
punish, you would find a sorrow and suffering enough to
disarm all your hostility

*H. W. Longfellow*

We write because we have to say what we believe
We discover what we believe because we write
All else of writing is but a searching for form,
a style, a technique, to show those beliefs
in an acceptable artistic manner.
When we succeed our hearts are on the stage
to touch the hearts and minds of the audiences.
It is an awesome experience.

*Unknown*

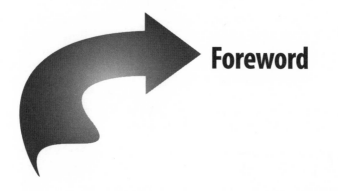

# Foreword

It isn't often one is asked to write a foreword to the second edition of a very popular book. Initially I didn't understand why Stewart would ask me, since I don't do conflict resolution or mediation of any sort. But I saw, in the subtitle, a word I like a lot: *collaboration*. So I sat down and read the book and then I understood my role.

You see, this book is about three things I value very highly. First, it is about a paradigm shift in resolving conflict. What Stewart is offering is a fundamentally new way to take a situation full of conflict, with the potential of "going to court," and turning it around so that both sides win.

Think about that for a minute: a system of rules and regulations that you can apply to almost any conflict—organizational, professional, personal—and end up with no conflict. In fact, end up with the two parties working together to make the world better for both.

Stewart takes you out of the courtroom, away from the lawyers, and gives you directions on how to find common ground and an agreement "in principle" which then guides you to building a roadmap to your mutual solution.

When you read his examples, you get this funny feeling: "I could have done that..." and then you think of a big conflict in your life where one of you, and usually both, end up dramatically dissatisfied.

I went through a major lawsuit in the 1990s, and I can tell you with certainty that if we had used Stewart's paradigm for conflict resolution it would have turned out very differently.

So, for just this one reason, Stewart's book is invaluable!

There is a second reason, and it has to do with the very important topic of innovation in the twenty-first century. My research into innovation tells me that much of it is going to be driven by differences, the combination of differences.

I call these kinds of innovations "innovations at the verge." A verge is the place where one thing and something very different meet. The verge provides a huge opportunity to combine ideas from vastly different industries and fields and cultures into powerful new innovations.

But—and this is a very big but—you will absolutely have to know how to collaborate at the highest order to be successful in this kind of innovation. Can you imagine taking an idea from a pharmaceutical company and adapting it with an idea from a concrete manufacturing company to create a verge innovation? Well, it will be combinations like that, and even stranger, that are going to drive the twenty-first century.

Stewart's book is the blueprint for how to act to achieve that kind of collaboration! If you want to be innovative at the verge, you have to know how to deal with differences. Stewart shows you how to do that.

The third reason I delight in Stewart's book is simple: it is a new vision for the world. I think visionary ideas are crucial to successful futures. Stewart is providing a vision, and a paradigm to support the vision, for how we can all get along a lot better.

Since I finished reading Stewart's book, I find myself building partnerships in a new way. I'm sure you'll find the same.

*Joel Barker*
*Futurist, author, filmmaker*

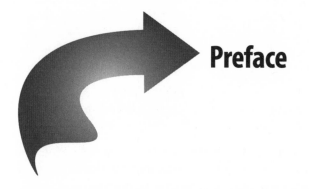

# Preface

During my second year of law school I had my first "real" lawyer's job. I was an intern at a local legal services clinic. On my first day I was handed twenty-five cases "to work on." This would be my job for the semester. Three weeks later I asked the managing attorney for more cases. When he asked about the twenty-five he had given me, I told him that I had resolved them.

He was very surprised—and very curious. He asked how I had done it. I told him that I had reviewed the files, spoken to the clients, thought about a fair outcome and what needed to be done, called the attorney or agency on the other side, and reached a satisfactory resolution.

I knew nothing about being a lawyer. I had no inkling that the cases were difficult, needed to take a long time, or had to be handled in any particular way. With common sense and a "beginner's mind," I found the solution that worked best for all concerned. Simple? It was for me!

I spent the next twelve years becoming a "successful" lawyer—and becoming less effective at resolving matters. Then, feeling frustrated, anxious, and fearful, I stopped practicing law. I have been in "recovery" ever since, recovering what I knew about resolution when I started, discovering its component parts, and learning how to teach and model it for others.

As a young attorney, although I listened politely to more senior lawyers, I was surprised at the coaching I received.

Standard practice discouraged communication among the parties in conflict, communication that I had used in my legal services cases, communication essential for efficient resolution. Many lawyers were playing a very different game from the one my natural instincts chose.

Yet, I was fascinated with how the most effective judges and lawyers paid attention to people's real concerns. They knew what to honor and what to respect. They knew how to frame situations and condition people's expectations. They embodied a tradition that accommodated competing concerns and built consensus. Winning or losing was not the point of their work. Their game was resolution and getting people back to their lives.

I had a similar orientation, and this orientation, coupled with my belief that everyone had a lot to learn about conflict, focused me on trying to understand conflict, this pervasive aspect of life. Amid all the business and personal conflict, there was some clarity: We could do a lot better at managing conflict, and we could prevent conflict if we formed new business and personal relationships in a different way.

I am driven and motivated to use resources efficiently, to minimize the emotional fallout from conflict, and to build sustainable collaborations. This book shares what I have learned from observation, study, and reflection. That journey continues.

## My Objectives

I have specific goals for this book:

1. Change your thinking about conflict. By providing a new set of principles and values, I would like you to shift from thinking about problems, fighting, and breakdowns to thinking about collaboration, engagement, learning, creativity, and the opportunity for creating value.

2. Provide a conversational model for agreement and resolution that enables you to develop the craft of helping people create sustainable collaborations. This model consists of specific, tangible steps for you to follow when conflict is present in any situation or when you start new professional or personal relationships.

3. Inspire you to develop a new perspective toward conflict. With this new perspective you could prevent the emotional trigger, the cost of unproductive energy, and the waste of resources. You would know that no matter how hopeless it seems, no matter how strong the emotional impulse to fight and win, resolution could be discovered within any situation.

4. Steward a mind-set of resolution. I want you to learn a model that fosters dignity and integrity; optimizes your resources; and allows all concerns to be voiced, honored, and woven into the resolution.

5. Foster a culture based on principles and practices of resolution and agreement. I hope the book motivates you to become a "resolutionary" in your life and a leader of others in practicing resolution, while at the same time appreciating the richness that the creative tension of differences provides.

6. Enable you to take personal responsibility for dealing with the opportunity of conflict, diversity, and disagreement.

This last goal is critical. We are living at a time of great opportunity. We can thrive if we design a world order that provides stability, optimizes natural resources, preserves the environment, controls population, and shifts our thinking from rights and entitlements to service and responsibility.

This process starts with each individual. You must tend your own garden. As a first step I encourage you to develop a spirit of resolution. Given our shrinking planet and the increasing transactions of our global village, learning to take responsibility for effective collaborations and resolving the inevitable conflicts is essential.

Now is the time to start working together more effectively!

## The Contents

This book is based on four premises:

1. *Conflict is expensive in many ways.*

2. *Efficient conflict resolution requires a new paradigm of collaboration grounded on ten principles* (delineated in Part II).

3. *Efficient conflict resolution requires using a new systematic approach—a model that is applied consistently and that reinforces the new paradigm through routine use.*

4. *The resolution of conflict using the model returns you to productive living and functional relationships.*

Part I of the book sets out its context. Chapter 1 explains what resolution is and why it is so valuable. Chapter 2 details the ways that conflict is expensive—the great individual and collective cost we incur on a daily basis as we work within the standard ways of handling conflict. I list, illustrate, and explain the cost of conflict so you can appreciate the huge expense. You see that, under current practices, "winners" are losing. Capitalist culture is based on economics and profit. I hope recognition of all the costs will motivate you to use new practices.

Part II shares a case study that introduces the model for

resolution (Chapter 3) and gives an overview of the steps in the model (Chapter 4).

Part III explains the principles (new thinking) for resolving conflict. Current practices are based on an underlying set of beliefs, beliefs that may have served you in a world based on power and control. That world, I sense, is fading, and it's time to adjust your thinking. The new principles reflect current, more enlightened, thought. These principles are the foundation for new practices of the resolution model.

Part IV provides a more detailed explanation of the resolution model introduced in Part II. Part IV also demonstrates the model in action, embodying the values of the new principles. It shares some of the results that have been achieved by following the model.

Part V addresses how the new resolution principles and model fit within current standard ways of resolving conflict. It also introduces the experts available to help you use the new principles and model—what they do and how to choose one.

Part VI provides a peek into what it can be like if we follow the principles and practices of resolution.

## How This Book Will Help You

The book is written for many groups. Everyone looking for a way to reduce the stress involved in collaborating with others, personally and in business, will find value. People who work with and for others will learn how to clarify their employment relationships.

For executives, managers, human resource and training personnel, business owners, and employees who must do more with less, this book will help increase productivity and improve communication and coordination among intercompany and intracompany teams.[1]

Entrepreneurs and business developers who must build "virtual organizations" will find this book useful. For consultants, lawyers, architects, and accountants (whose business depends on satisfied clients), this book will provide tools for clearly articulating expectations and constructing sound business relationships from the beginning. For managers, executives, mediators, lawyers, and psychologists (the increasing cadre working in the field of conflict resolution), this book provides new tools and insights.

I hope that managers and organizational development consultants will use the models as the foundation for building and changing organizational cultures. I believe that culture reflects the quality and character of organizational relationships. And the quality and character of organizational relationships reflect the nature and quality of the web of implicit and explicit agreements that are the foundation and glue of organizational relationships. Organizational relationships, both internal and external, reflect and embody the culture. The sum of relationships is the culture!

People who desire social change will embrace the model. Individuals seeking formulas for more effective use of societal resources will value the way resources can be conserved. Folks who bristle at litigiousness will see that the number of lawsuits can be reduced if we adopt the new principles as primary values.

Consumers of legal services, and those who are afraid of legal services, will see potential for huge financial and emotional savings. People looking for a professional who will enter into a more heartfelt relationship based on a shared covenant will learn to identify such professionals and the standards that can be used to formulate a satisfactory and predictable collaboration-based relationship.

Married people, family members, and those in other partnerships can construct agreements to guide them to deeper connection, greater understanding, and less stressful relationships.

## Beginner's Mind

Unfortunately, your impatience is likely to trump your desire to do things differently, so please be patient during the learning process. Please take on the dignity of a "beginner's mind" as you try the new practices. Most of you want to be experts immediately. You want to conquer the expert slopes on the mountain, master the new software, or take off on your new computer with little practice. Cut yourself some slack in gaining comfort and competence with the new practices. It will be worth it.

Following the principles and the model will enhance the quality of your life, the lives of those around you, and the culture of your various communities. The principles embody values that we all want to embrace. The model is simple, but applying it is challenging. Using new practices and developing new habits requires mindfulness, commitment, and repetition. As you acquire competence, you will become artful in discerning how much formal attention to the steps in the model some situations require, and what steps are not necessary in other situations. At the beginning I suggest that you practice using every step. That will help you internalize all the principles and practices.

After the first edition was released, I realized a few critical components that contribute to comprehensive understanding of "sustainable collaboration" did not get the attention they deserved. I am grateful to have the privilege of supplementing the book with the hindsight of ten years and a great deal of client and audience feedback. I hope you appreciate the utility of the changes as we navigate through a very challenging period of history. Twelve years ago I knew we had a universal problem. Our capacity to engage in civil discourse and dialogue, and to prevent or resolve conflict productively in critical public conversations, was sorely lacking. Unfortunately the last 12 years have not demonstrated progress. And the stakes are now higher!

This edition is motivated by a great sense of urgency. I just finished reading a marvelous book by David Korten called *Agenda for a New Economy: From Phantom Wealth to Real Wealth.* As we plod through a great economic meltdown I find myself reflecting on the public dialogue, or lack thereof, of the past dozen years. My assessment: Our leaders should all be fired for not taking care of the people's business. Our politicians behave as if it were the 1950s and all we have to do is to return to peacetime prosperity.

Instead of real dialogue about the pressing and urgent challenges we face—like terrorism, 9/11, Social Security, race relations, financial disparity, and climate change—our leaders continue lining up combatively along party lines no matter what proposal is put on the table. I can already see it happening with the new President's economic bailout, even within his own party. Rather than sitting down, exchanging ideas, and exploring common ground for some greater good, our leaders push forward with the ultimate antithesis of diplomacy and tact, engaging in a never-ending and debilitating game of "Gotcha!"

I can't help thinking that if our leaders had engaged in dialogue about matters of real substance we might have been able to focus on the pressing issues that continue to confront us. While Washington was playing politics, Social Security, Medicare, Iraq, Afghanistan, Fanny Mae, Freddie Mac, and Wall Street were ignored. And we are all picking up the tab for that.

A few years ago I was invited to speak to a group called Center City Proprietors Association (CCPA), the small business trade association for the city of Philadelphia. A couple of weeks beforehand, my friend Krista Bard, president of CCPA, asked if I would speak to the class of her ten-year-old son Alex when I was in Philadelphia. I said absolutely yes. A few days later I spoke with Alex's teacher and she told me that, in the wake of 9/11, the class had been working on something called "The Peace Table." The teacher was using it as a vehicle to keep the kids engaged in creating conversational tools for resolving conflict when questions arose about why the twin towers were targeted.

The evening before meeting the class I was still not sure what I was going to do with them, so I consulted Krista. She suggested that I do the same thing as I had done with the adults. So that's what I did.

Doing my best Mister Rogers imitation in a chair designed for a ten-year-old, I asked the kids what they use when they listen. The adults had hesitated. No such hesitation with the kids. A hand went up immediately and the first response was "my heart!" Krista and I looked at each other with wide eyes.

My immediate insight was that it does not need to take multiple generations to change mass consciousness and the requisite skill sets around conflict and collaboration. We just have to begin a massive educational campaign that provides alternative ways of thinking before kids are corrupted. Terrorists are not born, they are made by indoctrination. Partisan debaters—conservatives, liberals, radicals—are also made. I know we have the capacity to do much better!

Unfortunately, when "No Child Left Behind" became the banner for educational curricula, all else was dropped. My colleague, a noted specialist who wrote both kids' books and programs for conflict resolution, told me that all funds had evaporated. She had to go back to classroom teaching after spending years traveling the country teaching teachers and those who teach them.

How did we get here, and how can we get out of here? That is the context from which I write. What most people do not realize is that the skills presented in this book are tools that are essential for democratic participation. I believe that as a civilization we are tottering on a dangerous precipice. To resolve many of our great challenges we must be able to engage in thoughtful and authentic dialogue. We have conquered outer space; our big challenge is conquering "inner space." Given our current military capacity for destruction, if we cannot make the mental shift to fully engage in authentic conversation we risk the end of life as we know it.

The planet will survive. I'm not sure about our species!

I think learning the mindset, practices, and models set forth in this book is urgent. If we can develop our capacity to speak with each other we will be better able to connect with each other, and better able to address our pressing concerns. All else is moving deck chairs around on the Titanic.

As we move through the current economic crisis, many are suggesting the need for large-scale systemic change. A colleague, Christopher Avery, author of *Teamwork Is an Individual Skill*, recently labeled our current time as The Great Reckoning. I think the label is accurate. Given this time of reckoning, it seems important that we embrace communication and dialogue as essential to participating effectively in the democratic process. The bad news is that we have no choice but to engage, in part because people are sufficiently frightened. The good news is that there are tools available. I believe people will embrace new ways of interacting, and I hope you find some of them on the pages that follow.

## Acknowledgments

Inspiration for this book came from many sources. Gus Lee, the author of *China Boy*, was critical. As director of the Office of Education of the State Bar of California, he reviewed a script I wrote for a mediation video and said, "You have a very important message to deliver to the public. I want you to write a book."

From my parents, Adeline and Meyer, I learned about values, ethics, and integrity. They told me to find what I loved and success would follow. Susan Howard taught me to believe I was capable of accomplishing anything I wanted. John Haynes demonstrated the mood and process of mediation. I learned about leadership and resolution—my best work—from Marsha Shenk, who helped uncover the idea of "agreements for results." Bud Seith personified male mothering. Marty Africa is a daily demonstration of courage, perseverance, responsibility, and commitment; I thank her for shelter in the storm. From my brothers Peter, Bill, Larry, Cliff, and Steve, I learned the joy of camaraderie. My sister Sharron has taught me about acceptance. I thank Tish for her joy. I thank David for being there, and for the example that he is. Heartfelt gratitude for the endorsers of this book, and to Joel Barker for the great foreword.

Thanks to the community of Berrett-Koehler authors, who are working to make a world that works for all. I thank Steve Piersanti, the founder of Berrett-Koehler, for recognizing the value of this project. His vision and nurturing of my ideas has been an extraordinary gift. Laurie Harper of the Sebastian Agency falls in that category. I thank Phillip Heller, Jeffrey Kulick, Annette Simmons, and Paul Wright, the readers who reviewed the manuscript, for their thoughtful comments. Special thanks to Charlie Dorris, Barbara Kimmel, and Judy Johnstone for their careful editing, and to Detta Penna for her artful design work. I thank my clients and all who have attended my courses for their contributions to this body of work, and I thank the entire Berrett-Koehler staff for getting it out.

Most of all I acknowledge you, the reader. Thank you for your "resolve" to grow and to make your life—and the lives of those around you—more peaceful.

*Stewart Levine*
*February 2009*

# Part I

# The Value
# of Resolution

# 1

# Resolution: Getting Beyond Conflict, Compromise, and Settlement

> Through dialogue even the most un-resolvable conflicts can be worked out and everyone wins. The process did not include litigation or the emotional roller coaster ride that accompanies most conflicts. It was a delightful experience.
>
> *Bill Brown, President, Influence Communications*

I remember being surprised when told that settlement of a lawsuit is often characterized by thinking that "if both sides are unhappy, you probably have a good settlement." Resolution is much better than settling! Resolution provides relief and completeness. The situation no longer gnaws at your gut.

The most fitting dictionary definitions of resolution are: (1) the act of unraveling a perplexing question or problem; (2) solution; and (3) removal or disappearance, as in the disappearance of a tumor.

The third is the most important, even though often aspira-
tional. It means "as if it never happened." The gnawing effect I
call "internal chatter" has disappeared. The lack of chatter frees
you to focus energy and attention on the present. If you've ever
had a back injury, poison ivy, or a broken bone, you know what
I mean. Something is resolved when the injury or illness does
not impede the present moment.

This is important. You don't want to keep dealing with the
current impact of yesterday's conflict. The effect may consist
of holding anger or resentment, or thinking the result or compromise was unfair. Perhaps you compromised to get the situation behind you, or you deferred to someone else's decision.

Although at times I have tried not to, for more than 25
years—as a lawyer, mediator, consultant, and trainer—I have
practiced a resolutionary[3] attitude, one that looks for the fair
outcome from everyone's perspective. Whether you are a
hired advocate or you have a personal stake in the outcome,
you can adopt an "attitude of resolution." Evaluating the situation through the lens of resolution, you become an observer
of what might be fair to everyone in the situation, even if you
are directly involved. Standing in other's shoes provides the
critical perspective. The attitude of resolution is a skill you can
cultivate by being aware, reserving your own judgments, and
asking yourself if there is another solution that would serve
everyone's long- and short-term interests. It takes practice to
develop this new habit of thinking, but I have found this orientation far more useful than trying to win.

## Why Resolution?

Have you ever met someone who could not stop talking about
something that happened in the past? It pervades their life as
if it happened yesterday, although it may have taken place 20

years ago. They are stuck in the past, cut off from the ability to fully participate in their unfolding life.

Conflict has an emotional cost that remains after the battle is over. Win or lose, the scars may be with you for the rest of your life. Some people spend their lives focusing on the promotion they "lost," the business they "lost," the divorce they "lost," the project they "lost." This tunnel vision keeps them locked in the grip of their own anger.

They might even have "won," but they have not healed the real cause of the conflict—a breakdown in a relationship that was valuable enough for them to invest emotional energy in a battle. They never completed grieving and they still carry the emotional suffering. They never "resolved" the real issue. They may never even have identified it! Our current ways of thinking that focus on winning guarantee a cost: suffering. The small battles between partners, parents and children, and employees and bosses take a significant toll.

Productivity and satisfaction, in business and personal relationships, come from our ability to collaborate with others. When you are resolved, you can fully focus on the tasks at hand. Your efforts are undiluted. Unresolved conflict, on the other hand, is an impediment to productivity and to satisfying, functional relationships. In today's world of "knowledge work," focus and creativity are essential. It's impossible to be fully productive when you are angry. That's why resolving the situation that's sapping your strength and attention is very important.

It is equally important to have a sense of resolve when you start any new collaboration or relationship. You collaborate with others by reaching agreements. Your dependence on others is based on an intricate, pervasive web of agreements. Sometimes these agreements are explicit, but often they are implicit. Your collaboration will be stronger when you can recognize the implicit agreements within it. When you start out with uncertainty, or come into conflict during a project, you experience the cost of not being resolved from the outset. You also realize how inadequate your agreement-making and conflict-resolution tools are. Even though making agreements and resolving conflicts are essential life skills for working with others, they have not been taught to most of us.

Many current practices for resolving conflicts and starting collaborative relationships hinder us because of the way we were programmed to think, and because of the standard systems and practices in place. This book provides you with the following new tools:

1. Ten Principles of a new paradigm—a new way of thinking about conflict resolution.

2. The Cycle of Resolution, a seven-step model for preventing and resolving conflict that is a road map of new behaviors.

These ten principles and this seven-step model will maximize your ability to resolve conflict and achieve desired results in any business or personal relationship.

### The Value of Resolution at Work

As organizations cut costs, differentiate products, and streamline productivity, people need to work within increasingly complex webs of face-to-face and virtual collaboration toward common goals. They need tools that foster collaboration in the face of distance and differences of opinion and "culture." Rather than being angry and stuck, you must learn skills that foster resolution and quickly return you to productivity. This book presents the model for collaborative conversations that result in getting more done with fewer resources. This book reveals how agreement—the final step of resolving a conflict or the first step in the beginning of a new relationship—is an ongoing process, and that conflict and diverse opinions are opportunities for creativity and innovation. You will learn how to establish agreements based on deep heartfelt connection—agreements based on covenant.

Some of the benefits of establishing agreements based on covenant include:

Establishing shared vision of senior management

Improving teamwork

Creating partnership

Motivating participation

Including diverse perspectives and opinions

Using differences productively

Coordinating with external teammates

Using resources efficiently

Communicating more effectively

Building self-managing, high-performance teams

Forging consensus quickly

Fostering an environment of learning and growth

Promoting continual improvement

Capitalizing on the advantages of virtual organizations

Providing a more formal model of communication essential for effective virtual collaboration.

### *The Value of Resolution at Home*

In addition to their applications in workplace settings, the tools in this book will unlock more satisfying and intimate personal relationships within marriages, families, and less traditional partnerships that are part of our diverse social fabric. Because we usually think about personal relationships from an emotional and romantic perspective, it is difficult to accept that a linear process for resolving conflict and constructing agreements with specific promises about behavior will be helpful in producing more satisfying intimate relationships. My own experience leads me to suggest you bring the tools of this book into your personal life.

## The Big Picture

One primary challenge in getting to resolution is reaching an agreement in principle—a broad understanding of what the resolution will be. Once you have an agreement in principle, the heavy lifting is done. Filling in the details of a new agreement can be an enjoyable exercise in visionary thinking. You get to an agreement in principle when you cross a self-imposed emotional barrier and can let go of a position you have taken. For most people, this is not easy. It may require going against a lifetime of dealing with conflict in a different way. The steps of the model are designed to get you beyond this hurdle.[2]

Getting beyond the emotional barrier is not like personal therapy. The internal work is accomplished as a result of *new thinking* (adopting the values of the ten principles) and *new actions* (following the steps of the model). Every step of the model contributes to resolution by making you speak your thoughts, feelings, and perceptions about the conflict. Once your story is articulated and no longer purely emotional, you and others can deal with it.

Although the steps of the model seem linear, getting to resolution is not a linear process. Mechanically going through the steps will not lead to resolution unless you have embraced the values of the ten principles. Once you embrace the principles, you have embraced the model's first step, the Attitude of Resolution. Each successive step takes you toward resolution by making you go deeper into the personal, emotional, and human aspects of the conflict. You don't have to say yes to the principles because they feel good, seem right, or are morally or politically correct. It's fine to buy in because the cost of remaining in the conflict is too great. What is important is to get into the personal, emotional, and human aspects of the conflict. Regardless of what you *say* the conflict is about, the conflict is held as an emotional presence between you and at least one other person.

The new model provides a systematic approach. When you learn something new, it is important to have standard practices to follow. Standards provide guidance as you learn the new skill. When you learn to ski, drive a car, or fly an airplane, you put in place fundamentals that become unconscious habits. The model provides these fundamentals. Using the model develops habit and competence, and you discover the value of the principles. When you gain competence you will start to develop your own artistry—innovations within the standard practices. Once you internalize the principles and steps, resolution can happen quickly!

## Personal Responsibility for the Value of Resolution

Most of us avoid taking personal responsibility for conflict resolution. Even though our culture is litigious, we lack the courage to connect deeply with others and we personally avoid confrontation. If we have a disagreement in a business transaction or with a neighbor, we may let a lawyer take care of it. If we have emotional conflict, we may visit a therapist or counselor who (we hope) will tell us what to do.

The symptoms of conflict are stress, pain, and discomfort. When you take personal responsibility, you can impact the cause of the pain much faster than if you ask someone else to resolve the situation for you. Being responsible requires being open and vulnerable. If you are unwilling or unable to be authentic about your feelings, you may be quick to give up responsibility, and instead take false safety and security behind a more sterile, professional process. In doing that, you give up the potential of addressing your real concerns, getting to the core of the conflict, and reaching resolution.

Delegating conflict resolution to professionals who know how to diagnose and resolve your problems is a culturally learned response. But delegation compromises us when the professionals believe they are experts better equipped to make the key decisions that affect the core of our lives. Conflicts are filled with our feelings, and the professional to whom we hand the conflict does not have to live with the results of the resolutions.

This book is a call for personal responsibility. It asks you to adopt new practices, and to assume a new attitude in the world. It requests that you take personal responsibility for dealing with conflicts, differences, and disagreement, and that you become **ResponseAble.** Giving the process away deprives you of the satisfaction of "getting to resolution." You are uniquely capable of designing the best resolution and you will have the energy for follow-through because you own the solution. By being involved you derive value, strength, and the sense of self that full participation provides. Of course, there will be times when you need help. This book provides the guidance you may need.

## Learning New Behaviors

This book is a learning tool. My overriding concern is that you learn new thinking and new behaviors, new practices that will improve your professional and personal life. If you keep doing the same thing, you will keep getting the same results. Learning is the ability to take new actions to achieve new results. Unless you implement new behaviors, you have not learned anything. Resolution is simple, but it is not easy. This book will not be hard to understand. Your life experience has taught you many of the skills you need to master the art of resolution. The challenge is implementation—developing the habit of living the principles and behaviors on a daily basis.

In addition to my own experience, as background research for the first edition I spoke with more than a hundred senior conflict resolution professionals. Their insights validated many of the ideas in the book. And the ideas have been further validated by my experience over the last ten years. The stories in the book are true, although some of them are composites. They have been disguised to cloak the identity of individuals and organizations. You can be both facilitator and participant by internalizing the model and learning to become an observer of your situation. A goal of the book is for you to become "meta" to the situation—that is, you are outside or above it. I do it all the time, and you can too. The resolution principles and model can also be used for third-party interventions—when you try to help friends or co-workers resolve a conflict in which you are not personally involved, or as manager when you have direct responsibility.

I am inspired by the aim of resolution. I hope to inspire you. *Getting to Resolution* will teach you about patience, inquiry, learning, and expanding your perspective. The power and integrity of resolution leads to outcomes you cannot invent yourself. It's the difference between the sound of one hand clapping and two!

*Getting to Resolution* helps you understand what you already know about conflict. It shows you a simpler, more effective approach to reaching, modifying, and maintaining collaborative agreements, a key to your professional and personal success.

## Summary

- Resolution is taking care of conflict so that there are no lingering aftereffects. It is better than compromising because the cost of the aftereffects is less.

- The key challenge is reaching agreements in principle. This becomes easier when we adopt the principles of Resolutionary Thinking and engage in the dialogues that the Cycle of Resolution prescribes.

- Resolution has great value at work, at home, and within yourself. It is a skill you can learn by developing the habit of the new practices.

## Reflections

- How was conflict handled when you were a child?

- Have you adopted, without consciously choosing, the patterns you saw as a child? Do those patterns serve you?

- How do the ways you handle conflict make difficult situations worse?

- What would it be like if you could behave in ways that lead to the results you really wanted? How might your life be different?

# 2

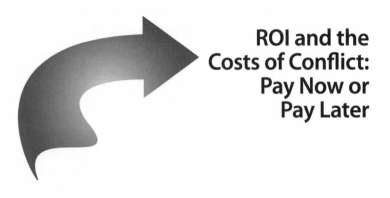

# ROI and the Costs of Conflict: Pay Now or Pay Later

I appreciate being able to handle this matter without investing any more time, effort, and money than was necessary.

*Karl Bareither, President, Family Business Consultants*

In 2006, 17.3 million civil actions were filed in state courts and in 2007, 1.12 million civil cases were filed in federal courts of the United States. You can imagine the cost of those lawsuits.[4] I once read that 20% of Fortune 500 senior executives' time is spent in litigation-related activities. Imagine the tally that adds up to. It's commonplace for legal fees to exceed the value of the amount at stake. Years ago, if a situation had more than $100,000 at stake, litigation was a viable alternative. Today the benchmark is $1 million and growing quickly. Old thinking is very costly!

Although the use of Alternative Dispute Resolution (ADR) is growing, the cost of conflict is a resource drain of huge proportion, and a source of great unhappiness and discomfort.

## Why So Expensive?

Traditional court systems, which many think of as the usual way of resolving conflicts, do not foster resolution. Their operative premise is that someone will win. Unfortunately, our dispute resolution machinery often fuels the fire of conflict and impedes resolution. Worse, while engaged in the conflict resolution process, your productive activity, what your life is really about, is diluted. The system does not foster resolutions that address the underlying sources of conflict—breakdowns in relationship. The process is not designed to get people back to an optimal state of productivity.

The current formal system embodies struggle, control, and a survival-of-the-fittest mentality. It is based on dialectic, right/wrong, either/or patterns that originated in Aristotelian logic. Even though we live in a densely populated, rapidly changing technological world that cries out for systems that foster collaboration, individuals and institutions tenaciously cling to old habits.

Elected representatives, often lawyers, to whom we cede control, sometimes believe that we can legislate ways of treating each other. Mostly for personal or political reasons they often have a knee-jerk response to enact a new rule or regulation in response to a problem. This does not work! Standards essential for a functional social fabric cannot be legislated. What's missing are the bedrock ethics and values that traditionally were taught by the educational community and religious institutions, and fostered in extended families. These values have become clouded in our me-oriented modern, mobile, sound-bite techno-society.

Because family structures and religious institutions have become so fragmented, we no longer rely on them to provide an education of core values. Many people seek external standards that will tell them what to do. People often have little ground-ing in collaborative skills. Real partnership flows from within the covenant-type relationships that community, family, and religious institutions have traditionally demanded and fostered. Many people have no role models and sadly, in many instances, don't know how to treat each other from within a common covenant.

Noted futurist Alvin Toffler has said that "the place we need really imaginative new ideas is in conflict theory. That's true with respect to war and peace, but also it's true domesti-cally. The real weakness throughout the country is the lack of conflict resolution methods other than litigation and guns."[5] Although there had been a great deal of nominal change by way of the ADR movement, the basic premise is still adver-sarial and Toffler is on track. The problem is caused by both the aspects of today's conflict resolution system and the way that it is administered. This includes:

- Increase in the body of statuary and case law reflecting the growing numbers of lawyers, and complex transactions requiring regulation.

- Commercialization of the legal tradition fostered by competition and advertising.

- Growing reliance on counselors and therapists who care for our internal conflict and feed our conflict-avoidance mentality.

- Breakdown of trust and the inability to assess the value of, or need for, specific actions that therapists or lawyers take (evidenced by growing malpractice claims).

- Attorneys' conflict of interest because their practice of hourly billing results in a devotion to process, not results.

- The growth of the contingent fee and a class of cases in which there is nothing to lose by taking a chance.

- The legal, economic, and emotional minefields of the litigation process.

- The myth of finding truth and justice in a courtroom, a myth that has been perpetuated by the role models celebrated on TV.

These reasons are symptoms. They evidence a breakdown in the covenants of trust between people who are members of the same "community." They point to a lack of communication. People are focusing on themselves. They are concerned about their rights and entitlements without thinking about their responsibilities toward others. This all flows from the win/lose systems and practices that are in place.

Many people are looking for guideposts and rules that will tell them how to treat each other. This requires new practices and new ways of thinking, which are the subject of this book. Before discussing them, let's examine the cost of doing things the way they are done now. As we review the many different costs, imagine how much more you might accomplish if you could harness the resources expended, the money and energy used in the battle of traditional conflict resolution. Imagine using those resources to produce the outcomes you want.

## The Cost of Conflict

The cost of conflict is composed of the following:

1. **Direct cost,** fees of lawyers and other professionals.
2. **Productivity cost,** value of lost time. The opportunity cost of what those involved would otherwise be producing
3. **Continuity cost,** loss of ongoing relationships including the "community" they embody.

4. **Emotional cost,** the pain of focusing on and being held hostage by our emotions.

It's important to identify the costs of conflict and examine some tangible examples. Recognizing the cost will, I hope, motivate change as quantifying the real cost demonstrates that there are no winners.

### Direct Costs

Because of an inability to face conflicts, many of you spend money you can't afford on professional gladiators hired to do your bidding. A divorce between two people whose only asset is their home can transform that residence into legal fees. The process brings out the worst in people who thought enough of each other to marry, but now can't even sit down and talk.

*An Empty Victory.* The Cobbs were involved in a lawsuit about water run-off and erosion problems that had not been disclosed to them when they purchased a new home from a professional relocation company. What started as their claim for $30,000 to repair water damage and reroute a driveway resulted in a four-year battle with legal fees of over $175,000 and engineering experts' fees of $25,000.

As the situation escalated, the Cobbs realized they had invested so much in professional fees they couldn't afford to lose their suit. They had to continue the fight. Mrs. Cobb was increasingly agitated because her husband had pushed the battle forward. The relocation company became more resolute in wanting to prove it was right. The company tied up the energy of its in-house counsel, two lawyers from a litigation firm, a senior company executive, and a real estate broker. All of this energy was focused on something that had happened four years earlier in which no one had intentionally done anything to harm anyone else. The end result was an empty victory. The Cobbs won, but the judge did not award them attorney fees— their only hope of getting even financially because the actual cost to repair the loss was only $30,000.

*Sally and Frank.* Sally and Frank were married for more than 20 years. While she was not committed to a divorce, Sally was clear that she could no longer tolerate things as they were. Sally finally mustered the courage to tell Frank her vision of the changes needed if the marriage were to continue. Frank became immovable. Sally and her closest friends tried to convince Frank that it was best for them to separate; maybe, during a cooling-off period with some distance between them, they could create a new foundation for their relationship. Frank could not hear the advice of his peers, professionals, or family.

After many unanswered requests for Frank to sit down and work out a solution, Sally filed for divorce. Frank dug in his heels. He cut off financial support. Although Frank was advised that to get the reconciliation he wanted he was better off leaving for a while, he chose to engage in a battle that could have no winners. Frank hired an attorney who mirrored his own attitude. They would not pay one dime or cooperate until ordered by a judge.

Sally and Frank ran up tens of thousands of dollars in lawyers' fees. Thousands were spent on psychological evaluations by therapists and by accountants who valued Frank's business. Each side had their own experts, as well as those appointed by the court.

Although part of the current paradigm, these fees are a waste of resources. The amount would have been better spent on setting up new households for Frank and Sally. The experts' fees could have been devoted to building self-esteem in the present and counseling for the transition. Instead, they were devoted to an already-dead past. For Sally and Frank, a simple process at the outset would have made the situation history.

### Productivity Cost

Time is a valuable, limited commodity. When people are focused on rehashing the past, they cannot create and produce value in the present. There are two aspects of this cost—direct loss and opportunity cost. The direct loss is the value of a person's time—what litigants should be earning but are not being paid because they are engaged in the conflict. The opportunity cost is the value the person might have produced if that energy had been focused on creation and innovation.

**Intellectual Property.** Two colleagues designed two innovative forms of management "technology." These processes were significant additions to the knowledge base about personal productivity and leadership. They battled for over a year about who owned the intellectual property they had developed. The productivity loss from their feud was enormous. Instead of giving many students and clients the value of what they discovered, their time was devoted to fighting. That direct loss was their loss in revenue. The opportunity cost consisted of the value of innovations that might have been developed during the conflict, and the value each student might have produced.

**Sally and Frank, Part 2.** In Sally and Frank's situation, Frank was focused on the conflict, not on his business; his capacity was diminished during the entire conflict because of his mental preoccupation. To create an example, if he earned $2,000 per week, he was completely out of work for six weeks of court time, and his capacity was diminished by 25% for the two-year period of litigation, the direct productivity loss would be $64,000.

| $2,000 | x | 6 weeks | | | = | $12,000 |
|---|---|---|---|---|---|---|
| $2,000 per week | x | 104 weeks | x | 25% | = | $52,000 |
| | | | | | | $64,000 |

The opportunity cost is harder to calculate, but probably Frank's attention to the divorce caused him to miss opportunities such as designing new profit centers for his business, capitalizing on special sales of merchandise, or expanding his operations.

### Continuity Cost

Continuity costs result from being stuck in the past and include such things as the loss of relationship and community.

**Lifelong Friends.** Mira and Angela were like sisters. They had grown up together and had married and raised children at the same time. They lived in the same community. They were enriched by the strength of their relationship. Hardly a day went by that they did not spend time together. Their connection was a lifeline, a great blessing for both of them. When their children entered high school, they decided it was time to go into business together.

They were children of the 1960s who had always sparked each other's creativity. Their lives had never been about accumulating wealth; they just wanted to hang out together. They opened a modern-day general store staffed by pleasant people. The casual mood of the shop was a respite from the cold experience of many retail establishments.

The store was an instant hit. They grew. They added a cafe. They opened a second and third store. Eight years later there were 23 outlets, and Mira and Angela were making more money than they dreamed possible. They got to spend most days together and were very happy. What a life! Their husbands and children joined the business. They were building a solid foundation.

Years before, Mira and Angela had pledged never to let money or possessions come between them. Unfortunately, their husbands had not taken the same vow. Mira's husband Alberto had worked in the financial services industry. The idea of taking the company public put dollar signs in his eyes. His early investigation revealed that Mira and Angela could each pocket $6 million by selling 40% of the company stock. Angela wanted nothing to do with investment bankers and the close scrutiny that federal regulators would bring. She was very concerned about losing the flavor of what had made them successful. But Alberto was hungry . . . aggressive . . . and greedy!

Greed can do amazing things to people. Alberto started to undermine the Mira/Angela team. He created a crack that turned into a huge chasm. Ramon, Angela's husband, tried to open a dialogue, but Alberto was too headstrong. He was intent on proving he was right, that not taking the company public would lead to its downfall. The mood that had made the company successful was lost. The spark was fading. Profits were falling. Angela stopped talking to Mira because she couldn't control Alberto. One after another, the stores were closed. Angela and Mira were alone. They never spoke again.

**Three Feet of Real Estate.** Joanne asked me to represent her in a lawsuit filed by her next door neighbor. For more than 30 years Joanne had treated a three-foot strip of property adjacent to her driveway as if she owned it. Joanne planted flowers and maintained the lawn. On a visual inspection it was obvious that the property belonged to her. One day, however, her neighbor Ruth required a survey as part of a refinancing. The survey revealed that technically the strip was owned by Ruth.

Because the relationship was cordial, I was surprised that no informal demand or letter had been sent by Ruth before the lawsuit. I reviewed the documents and replied to the suit. I suggested that Joanne meet with Ruth to discuss the situation. She agreed, but to Joanne's surprise Ruth refused to speak about the situation. Her attorney took a similar posture with me. I believed Joanne had an 80% chance of prevailing if we went to court because her long-term use of the land had never been protested. I told Joanne, however, that there was always risk in going to court and it would be wise to make a settlement offer. She agreed to do that. The other side refused to negotiate. We did go to court. The judge suggested a settlement. Again no response from Ruth. We won, but it was an empty victory.

Joanne found out that Ruth was acting on the advice of her attorney, including the refusal to communicate. Joanne could not let go of her anger. She felt like a criminal, even though she never had any evil intent and she had won the lawsuit. Two years later Joanne sold the home she loved. She could no longer stand the anger she felt whenever she looked at the strip of land.

*Brother and Sister.* Seth and Sarah had a bitter fight over their father's estate. Growing up, they had been close confidants. And even though distance grew between them because of a geographical separation, they remained devoted to each other. When their father died, however, they had a disagreement about family money that had been given to Seth to invest in a business. Was that money a gift or an advance on his inheritance? They were both partly correct in their positions and were both convinced they could win in court. They both lost the war. Seth and Sarah did not speak for 30 years. At the funeral of their brother Steve, they looked at each other and broke down in tears, knowing they could never regain what they had lost.

Most people do not realize that when a business has to replace a managerial-level employee it costs the organization between 1.5 and 2 times the annual salary to recruit, hire, train, and get a new employee fully functional. Consider that the next time you are thinking of firing someone.

### Emotional Cost

Sometimes there are situations you can't let go of: a fight with a spouse, boss, co-worker, neighbor, friend, partner, or the person who ran into your car. The emotions of anger, fear, and blame grip you and force a reaction that saps your current productive capacity. Instead of going about your business, you are riveted on the injustice done to you and the untoward behavior of the perpetrator. You are consumed with vengeance and desire to punish the wrongdoer. You expend energy on your anger in addition to the loss you already have suffered. All of this energy will never be recovered.

**The Revenge of the Past.** Randy finally received the promotion he was longing for. That was the good news. The bad news was his inability to focus on his job. He was going through a messy child custody battle with his ex-wife. That stirred up all of the anger he was holding about the past relationship. She wanted to mediate the dispute, but Randy was set on winning. Unfortunately he lost—his job. It was a position that required all of his attention. He missed two important deadlines because his mind was focused on the past.

**Sally and Frank, Part 3.** Sally and Frank remained embroiled in legal turmoil for almost two years. Sally had to go to court for every ounce of relief: to get Frank out of their marital home, to force him to provide basic support, and to get him to pay the mortgage. She won each little skirmish, but Sally and Frank, and their children, have suffered huge amounts of emotional trauma. Sally and Frank hardly speak to each other; their children are having very difficult teenage years; their respective parents, previously social friends, do not speak to each other; and they were paralyzed in getting on with their lives. They will never be the same.

Major life changes are never easy, but doing legal battle over issues that are essentially emotional is like playing baseball on an ice hockey rink. For the balance of their lives, Sally and Frank will suffer because they would not let go of the past. They will never be friends. Their children are scarred. You can't put a price tag on these emotional losses, but the cost is huge. What might have been a simple process turned into a situation in which the conflicts escalated and the pain, suffering, and scars are magnified.

### *Summary*

- Current attitudes and systems of conflict resolution foster conflict.

- Conflict is very expensive. It consists of the following, never to be recovered, costs: (1) direct cost—professional fees; (2) opportunity cost—what would otherwise be produced; (3) continuity cost—the loss of relationships and "community"; (4) emotional cost—the pain of being held prisoner by emotions.

## *Reflections*

- Think about the expensive conflicts in your own life.

- What was the direct cost? The cost of professionals? The opportunity cost? The emotional cost? The relationship cost?

- As you reflect on your situation, think about the different actions and results you might have had if you had taken a different tack.

- How might you do it differently next time? How would your life be different?

# Part II

# A Better Way of Resolving Conflict

*If resolution is so good, how do you get there, and what does it look like? Part II provides an introduction to the steps of the model of resolution and a case study of a successful application.*

# 3

# Two Brothers: Their Story of Resolution

I saw little hope in coming to a fair settlement. . . . Each of the others I had gotten advice from led me to believe the only solution was a court battle. . . . I found the resolution model representative of the concerns of a partner. . . . We each walked away with a feeling of winning.

*Bill Thomas, President, Integrated Promotions*

Sometimes new ways of doing things are not readily understood. They do not fit with the way our perceptual systems have been conditioned. We cannot see what we are not already expecting.

A classic illustration is the story Joel Barker tells about the watchmaking industry. Before quartz, the Swiss held about 95% of the market. In the early 1960s the Swiss R & D people presented their innovation, the quartz movement, to the barons of the Swiss watchmaking industry. The barons didn't get it. The innovation did not include a mainspring, moving parts, or jewels. It could not possibly be a timepiece. The Japanese saw it, and the rest is history.[6] You may have a similar response to the message of this book. I want to give you a look at the big picture first.

Here is a story that demonstrates the principles and model in action, brings the new paradigm alive, and—I hope—motivates you to embrace it.

## The Story of Two Brothers

Two brothers were running a family enterprise that their grandfather had started. The business was profitable, was well located, and had a fine reputation. Their city was growing and the economy was expanding. Life was good. The brothers each married and began to raise families.

Tom, the younger brother, wanted to expand the business. He hired a consultant and then asked his brother Bill to be his collaborator in growing the family enterprise. Trusting and open-minded, Bill listened carefully to his brother's ideas and to those of the consultant. There was a family legacy of integrity to uphold, and Bill was concerned about his brother's motives. After considerable reflection and some hesitancy, he agreed to support the new direction.

The consultant recommended hiring new people. One was an ambitious young man. Bill was not comfortable with him, but he did not take a stand out of respect for Tom's dreams. Bill was concerned about changing the character of their business. He was afraid Tom was following a darker part of himself. Bill thought his brother was acting like a boy seeing what he could get away with, not like a man providing value in the family tradition.

The ambitious young man convinced Tom that Bill wasn't aggressive enough and was impeding the company's growth. Bill's wife noticed that Bill wasn't sleeping and that there was trouble between the brothers where there had previously been great respect. Rather than providing more to their customers, or increasing the company's capacity so they could serve more people, the company began to exploit customers by giving less service and charging more. This was not the family ethic that had made Bill so proud. Tom was being dishonest with customers, making promises and delivering little. When the brothers argued, Bill pointed out that people actually needed to be protected from their company's behavior. Bill remembered his grandfather's warning: Know where to take a stand to preserve your reputation for integrity.

Bill saw his brother as being poisoned by greed and ambition. He asked Tom to reconsider his strategy in order to avoid the inevitable result—that they would lose their respected reputation and their business. Tom glibly dismissed him as naive and parochial. Bill decided to leave the company. His heavy heart left him no choice. He was unwilling to compromise his standards, and he could no longer live with his brother's actions. Tom could not hear what Bill was saying about integrity, standards, and family tradition.

### Conflict

It was necessary to reach a financial settlement about their partnership. The family business had to be divided, and one of the brothers' friends suggested they call me. I was not surprised that by the time they called Tom and Bill were militant. On the basis of preliminary advice and their personal understanding of how these situations play out, they were moving into the traditional system of "confliction." It was impossible for them to move forward. Each was locked in the posture of blaming the other, insisting he was right, his brother wrong. Proving "I am right" became the most important part of the conflict.

The brothers were steeling for a battle. They stopped talking to each other. Each consulted his own gladiator. There was no sign of being able to stand in the other's shoes, and no ability to be open and real about the situation. Their positions were polarized, and their feelings of great loss were not being recognized. They were beginning to defer to their professionals.

Meanwhile, business was at a virtual standstill. All energy was devoted to winning the battle. The struggle was about how much the business was worth and who would pay whom, when, and on what terms. No one was thinking about reaching a fair resolution, taking care of customers, or the future of the business. The pie they and their family had so painstakingly baked was crumbling.

Both brothers were living in the traditional way of thinking: They were framing their situation as a great problem with many issues, not as a business event that required creativity to accommodate everyone's concerns.

### *The Attitude of Resolution*

I focused on helping Bill and Tom see how continuing the battle would cost them time, money, emotional upset, a huge chunk of opportunity cost, and scars they would carry for the rest of their lives. Neither of them would be devoting time to the future; there would be no time free from the emotional baggage of the past. I sensed from separate conversations with each of them that preservation of brotherhood was a concern neither of them wanted to address or acknowledge. After I spoke to them, they understood that they would both be better off with a new agreement that was reached quickly. Neither could afford the financial, emotional, or spiritual cost of escalating acrimony. The message I sent them was their wake-up call:

If you go to court and continue to do battle, you will end up with a new agreement. The terms will be dictated by a judge who knows very little about your situation. The decision is likely to be far less workable for each of you than one that could be designed by both of you. Please consider what I am saying very carefully. Remember the wisdom of Solomon when he quickly resolved a custody dispute by suggesting that the child be cut in two. If we work together we can design the resolution that creates value for both of you. Otherwise, by the time the war ends the business will have little value, and you will lose each other.

After I discussed their expected resistance with each of them, the brothers were willing to meet together with me. They had become so upset they had nothing to lose. Getting people together is more than half the battle. Coming to the table holds the unspoken declaration "I want to resolve this matter."

When we met, tempers were hot. I thought it best to resolve the situation as quickly as possible. They agreed to continue one session until everything was addressed.

### Telling the Story

The first part of the day gave each brother the opportunity to tell his story. I reminded them that it might be important to preserve their brotherhood and that the cost of not reaching an agreement together would be enormous. Each listened carefully as the other spoke without interruption. For both, it was like having their day in court. They spoke what was in their hearts. This enflamed their anger, but it also provided catharsis. It gave me a sense of where the situation was at that moment and where it might be headed. I listened to what was being said, and I also listened to what was *not* being said.

## *Completion*

After the brothers had told their stories, I asked them a structured set of questions—a completion process that guided them across tender and volatile ground. Each spoke of being so frustrated and irritated by the other brother that it was impossible to be around him. Many harsh, almost unmentionable things were said. I facilitated the dialogue into areas of vulnerability that we all have about someone as familiar as a brother. Disappointment, shame, sorrow, and the loss of the family tradition were among these. The process was difficult, but it was also a great release. The open hostility started to diminish. They realized their camaraderie had been displaced by greed. Tears were shed, and some understanding began to surface.

When they saw what they had lost—unrealized expectations of separate visions for the future—they could grieve. This allowed them to let go and start to form a new vision for their separate futures without one another, what I call an agreement in principle.

## *New Agreement*

As the long day wore on, the brothers put their new vision of the future into an agreement. It contained what they wanted and what they would need from each other in their new business relationship. Most important, and crucial to their respective prosperity, they were both heading off on their own, using their resources to build a new future. They were no longer stuck in the past, fighting and wasting energy about what had already crumbled.

We did not just get the matter settled. We resolved the emotional issues and structured what their future relationship would be. Bill would move to another part of the state and start his own business. It was their intention to help each other have a successful business reflecting their particular values. Reaching a buy-out figure was not difficult once the emotions were addressed. They agreed not to compete with each other. Their measure of satisfaction was success in business and continuing brotherhood. Their fear was dishonoring their new agreement.

### *Resolution*

A new form of partnership was born. These "enemies" realized their brotherhood. They became colleagues, creditors, fellow travelers who had wisdom and experience to share. Most of all, they remained brothers. The details of the business agreement were not as important as having them quickly move into the future with minimal disruption and expense. They felt good to be resolved, back in action, and productive. The heartbreak could start healing.

I assumed the responsibility of keeping everyone accountable for satisfactory resolution. It's a matter of having the patience and determination to stay on track until the resolution appears. No matter how bleak the situation looks, you must keep swimming upstream, both guiding and allowing everyone to educate each other about what the optimal outcome might be. You must hold fast that resolution will happen. This can look like position and power, but it is really about faith.

### *Summary*

- This chapter contains an example of the Cycle of Resolution in action.
- The story demonstrates the value of seeing the bigger picture and recognizing what is being wasted in a situation.

- It provides some insight into the texture of resolution, as well as an example of what's possible and the value of a new perspective you can adopt.

- You can use the same process for yourself .

- The Cycle has wide application—both as to the situation, and as to who uses it.

### Reflections

- Think of a long-term relationship in which a situation of conflict was resolved by either your winning or your taking advantage of another.

- How did you feel after the thrill of victory wore thin?

- Did the situation come back to have consequences or repercussions you did not see when you won?

- Would resolution have been more enduring? Why? Why not?

# 4

## The Craft of Resolution: A Road Map for Resolving Conflict

If you want to succeed, strike out on new paths rather than travel the worn paths of accepted success.

*John D. Rockefeller*

We don't think about the web of agreements making up our lives until we think that a collaborator has violated an explicit or implicit agreement that we believed we had. Then the voice of our internal chatter gets louder. You would think that the skill of crafting clear agreements, because it is so basic to successful living, would be an element of our core curriculum, installed during our early educational process as part of our basic operating system. Unfortunately, we usually learn through suffering, when we realize we do not know what goes into an effective agreement.

At the outset of a transaction or relationship, it is important to be clear and detailed about where you are heading. Recently I asked Mark, a senior manager at Visa, to share his greatest challenge. He told me that he often observed people moving into action before they knew where they were going. He wanted people to be clear about their destination before they moved into action, otherwise they end up in places where they do not want to be. It's the difference between "Ready, fire, **aim!**" and "Ready, aim, **fire!**" In terms of the model of resolution, this concept is important for two reasons: (1) clarity on the front end of a new relationship minimizes conflict; and (2) the resolution of conflict is a new, clear agreement.

Mark's concerns are best illustrated in the classic story of the "Abilene Paradox." [7] Here's a brief version.

**Abilene Paradox.** Six people were sitting on a porch one hot August night about a hundred miles from Abilene, Texas. The temperature was 99°F and so was the humidity. So they decided to pile into a sedan without air-conditioning and headed over unpaved roads for Abilene to buy ice-cream. As they traveled, road dust wafted into the vehicle, coating their skin. They began sweating and became increasingly uncomfortable. Each wondered whose dumb idea it was to go to Abilene.

The trip back was no better. They became more agitated as they returned home. The internal din of "Whose dumb idea was it?" increased to a roar as they sweated and the ice cream melted, adding stickiness to the coat of dust. When they arrived home they piled out of the vehicle as quickly as they had piled in, bickering and finger pointing. As they quieted down, they began to see that no one had wanted to go to Abilene. Each had gone along for the ride, thinking it was a dumb idea but not wanting to say so.

How many trips to Abilene have you taken? Creating an effective agreement at the beginning of a relationship will save you many uncomfortable miles—or, as they said in the old oil filter commercials: "You can pay me now or pay me later!"

## A Universal Model for Working with Others

Dialogue *at the beginning* of a relationship prevents conflict and puts all people involved on the same page. The conversation builds partnership; everyone begins with the same vision in mind. The dialogue shines light on the transaction by articulating all the details. It maximizes the chance for everyone to obtain what they want.

Although there is a fine body of work on conflict theory suggesting principles that will get you to resolution, there is no easy-to-follow model that specifies what needs to be discussed and resolved to reach an effective agreement. From my experience as a lawyer and my work for business organizations I developed just such a model for anyone who wants to maximize a personal ability to have successful collaborations.

The model takes you through steps of a dialogue that lead to an effective agreement. It moves you through the inevitable conflicts, back to a state of resolution and productivity. Although the model is presented in a linear fashion, when you begin working with it, you will understand its artfulness and the "soft" edges of the steps in the process.

The following is a list of the steps followed by a short overview of each one; this corresponds to the illustration on the next page. Chapters 15 through 21 contain the detailed "how-to" for each step, along with illustrative stories and a more thorough explanation.

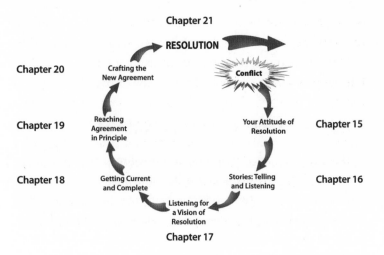

The seven steps of the resolution model, which I call the "Cycle of Resolution," are:

Step 1. Developing the Attitude of Resolution

Step 2. Telling Your Story

Step 3. Listening for a Preliminary Vision of Resolution

Step 4. Getting Current and Complete

Step 5. Seeing a Vision for the Future:
Agreement in Principle

Step 6. Crafting the New Agreement:
Making the Vision into Reality

Step 7. Resolution: When Your Agreement Becomes Reality

As you follow the discussion of each of the steps, remember the process the two brothers, Tom and Bill, went through in Chapter 3.

### *Step 1. Developing the Attitude of Resolution*

The Ten Principles that will be presented in Part III comprise the values that make up the attitude of resolution. This attitude is the place of beginning, a critical first step. It is not enough to go through the motions of the process mechanically without first cultivating the attitude or mood of resolution. This will not happen at once. It will take time to change the way you think. The beliefs and patterns you have about conflict took a long time to develop; they are deeply embedded and operate in unconscious ways. It will require intention to adopt new ways of thinking about collaborators and conflict, and new ways of communicating. This calls for faith and trust in yourself and in others. You can accomplish it. This is the foundational step. The goal is internalizing the principles of *resolutionary thinking*.

### Step 2. Telling Your Story

The second step is telling your story and listening to *all* the stories, including yours. It is about understanding and being understood, one of the seven habits of highly effective people that Steven Covey inspires us to cultivate.[8] There is great value in listening to the stories of others who are part of the situation. Looking for *the* truth in their story is not as important as honoring their authenticity and understanding *their* truth. Developing sharp listening skills enables you to understand another's view of reality. If you learn to listen with a careful ear and honor everyone's story about a situation, you take a big step toward getting to resolution.

### Step 3. Listening for a Preliminary Vision of Resolution

The third step is to listen and think about a resolution that honors all concerns in the situation. It is about shifting from the desire to get your way (win) to a vision that everyone can buy into because it comes from a sense of fairness. This initial vision may change as you gather more information. You must stay with the perspective that it is as important for "them" to get what they want as it is for you to get what you want. This was the sense I had when I resolved those cases in my law school clinical program. This is the thesis in Roger Dawson's work on "power negotiating"—the most powerful way to get what you want is to make sure that others get what they want.[9] The roots of the resolution come from believing in abundance—that there is enough for everyone. We are not playing in a zero sum game!

### *Step 4. Getting Current and Complete*

The fourth step demands saying difficult, sometimes gut-wrenching things. It is about articulating what usually goes unexpressed and escaping from the emotional and intellectual prisons that keep us locked in the past. It is a way to face the good and bad in any situation and to experience and grieve for the disappointment of unrealized expectations. It is a way to put all of the detail out on the table—and choose those remnants that can be used to weave a new tapestry of resolution.

### *Step 5. Seeing a Vision for the Future:*
### *Agreement in Principle*

Now that you have a preliminary vision, along with the information and emotional freedom provided by the completion process, you are ready for the fifth step—reaching an agreement in principle. Having looked at what other people need and noticing the cracks in your righteous position, you are ready to reach a general understanding of the resolution. This is the foundation of a new agreement. You let go of the desire for what you know will not work, and you focus on what will.

Your Agreement in Principle reflects the new era you are ready to step into.

### Step 6. Crafting the New Agreement: Making the Vision into Reality

In this step you put specifics onto the agreement in principle. You design and construct a detailed vision of the future. The key point: You have a map, a formula, for the dialogue that will maximize the potential for everyone to obtain their desired results. The more time you spend detailing the desired future, the greater the chance to realize it.

### Step 7. Resolution: When Your Agreement Becomes Reality

The seventh and final step is moving back into action. With a new agreement and a quiet, clear mind about the past, you can freely move forward, devoting your energy and intention to currently desired outcomes. You will have a new and profound sense of freedom because you have emptied yourself of the past and spoken all the "unspeakables." You have completed the past and constructed a clear picture of the future and the highway that will get you there. You will be empowered by the process. You are resolved.

### Summary

- This chapter introduces the Cycle of Resolution, a seven-step model and road map
- Chapters 15–21 will explain each step in greater detail, after you have been introduced to the principles (Chapters 5–14) that are the foundation of Step 1, the Attitude of Resolution.

## *Reflections*

- Make a choice to adopt the principles and practices suggested in this book.

- Select a few collaborations that are not quite what you would like them to be.

- Commit to try the model for 21 days, the time it takes to establish a new habit. Choose the date you will begin. Notice what happens!

# Part III

# Resolution: Ten Principles of Resolutionary Thinking

*The steps to resolution are of little value unless you embrace the underlying values driving the new practices. Part III explains the ten principles that make up the "new thinking" that is the foundation of the model.*

# Ten Principles of New Thinking

| OLD THINKING | NEW THINKING | CHAPTER |
|---|---|---|
| **1.** Scarcity | **1.** Believing in abundance | 5 |
| **2.** Wasting of resources | **2.** Creating partnership | 6 |
| **3.** Problems, issues, emotions | **3.** Being creative | 7 |
| **4.** Fostering conflict | **4.** Fostering sustainable collaboration | 8 |
| **5.** Righteous bravado, posturing | **5.** Becoming open | 9 |
| **6.** Short-term adversary | **6.** Forming long-term collaborations | 10 |
| **7.** Logic | **7.** Relying on feelings and intuition | 11 |
| **8.** Secrecy | **8.** Disclosing information and feelings | 12 |
| **9.** Winning | **9.** Learning throughout the resolution process | 13 |
| **10.** Deferring to professionals | **10.** Becoming *ResponseAble* | 14 |

# 5

**PRINCIPLE 1**
# Believing in
# Abundance

| OLD THINKING | NEW THINKING |
|---|---|
| *Scarcity* | *Believing in abundance* |

When you look at the world in a narrow way, how narrow it seems! . . . But when you look at it in a broad, generous, friendly spirit, what wonderful people you find in it.

*Horace Rutledge*

The first principle—abundance—is included in and foundational to all others. If you don't believe there is "enough"— enough for you to get what you want and for others to get what they want—resolution will be very difficult. If you believe there is enough, then following the other nine principles and the steps of the model will produce resolution. It will not always be easy, but it is that simple!

## Abundance: A Product of Creativity

Abundance is present in any situation as a reflection of your creative capacity. Your creative ideas are the source from which value emerges. I recently called a client who had not paid his bill. He said he did not have the money. Instead of becoming angry, I asked about whether there were any other services or property he might provide to compensate me for the value of my services. After speaking for a while, we realized he had some computer equipment worth twice the value of what I was owed that I needed and that he was not using. I was very pleased with the resolution, and so was he. This potential exists in every conflict. It's a matter of engaging in a productive dialogue so that what is needed to resolve the situation can be discovered or invented out of the creative potential that surrounds us all the time.

If the two brothers in Chapter 3 had remained narrowly focused on dividing the business, they never would have arrived at the place where their creative talent could benefit them. When they realized things were not working, they had a choice. They could fight about what they thought they had, or they could turn to each other and realize that, through their prior joint and individual creative efforts, they had reached the top of a mountain. From this vantage point each saw a new summit that he wanted to climb. The new summits were different, but there was no reason not to continue "partnering" with each other.

There is no law that says we both can't get to the top of the mountain of our dreams. Why hold a position that it must be a particular way. If you are willing to consider a larger universe of potential solutions, you may get much more than you expected.

## Abundance: The Creativity of Money

All profit, value, wealth, and accumulation result from the ideas of either one person or of a group of people combining their energy and talent. Think for a moment of a new business, a new team, or a community project that you were once part of. The value of the business, the contribution to the larger organization, or the benefit to the community came from someplace. The hi-tech revolution started as an idea in someone's mind. The creative energy of many people coming together and the innovations they have designed have made many millionaires, and a few billionaires. The source came from an unlimited supply of abundant potential. Before 1980 the whole domain of cell phones and PCs as personal productivity tools barely existed.

It's your choice! If you choose the principle of abundance when you come together to resolve a conflict, you can step into a field of enormous potential. It's not you or me; it's not us or them...it's you *and* me; we *and* they. No matter the situation, we can all have what we want if we tap into the abundant supply available to all of us. The resolution may look different than our initial expectation. So what? Remember, the glass is half full!

### *"AND" as the Operative Mindset*

**Liza and Kathy.** Liza and Kathy were partners in a successful consulting and training business. After ten years together they reached a crossroads. The question they faced was whether to hire additional consultants or to retain their current size and select higher-quality projects.

Liza was clear that the best course was selecting bigger clients. She did not want all the headaches of having employees.

Kathy was certain about hiring a few more consultants to leverage their existing business. These two intelligent, competent individuals were both sure of their own direction. Each was correct about the right path—for her. But that was not the question. The question was what they should do for the business and for their partnership.

As time passed, Liza and Kathy became resentful of each other's position. Even though they loved their work and their clients, each was wasting brain space with thoughts of how to manipulate the situation to her advantage. The crisis came to a head when Kathy found out Liza turned down a request to train a multi-division computer manufacturer in their proprietary communication model; it was not a high-quality prospect in Liza's opinion. Kathy was crazed by Liza's decision; Liza was unfazed by Kathy's outrage. Liza believed she had made the right decision. She had, for Liza.

After three days of lost productivity and not speaking to Liza, Kathy called me. I asked her what she wanted. Kathy's response was typical. She just wanted to put this behind them and get back to work. Liza had the same response when I spoke to her. For both of them the pain was so great that having a particular resolution was not as important as resolution itself. I let them think about that over the weekend and scheduled a meeting for Monday morning.

On Monday I asked if they could live with the fact that they were both right. They said yes, if they could get back to work! I asked them to design the structure of the business they wanted to operate. I asked them to exchange plans and let me know how they would participate in the other's plan. Then each chose her roles. I asked if there was a reason they couldn't live with the jobs they had selected in the other's design. They were OK with their roles. Good, I said. You have worked this out.

What was their plan? Kathy managed the expanded number of consultants, and Liza focused on more senior projects. They both returned to the joy, productivity, and fulfillment that made the partnership great. They did not compromise. Each had her concerns taken care of. This is a good example of how often we step into an either/or mind-set—either you get yours, or I get mine. It is important to remember that if you refuse to see the other person as the enemy and you each engage your creativity, often everyone can have what they want. Seeing the world as abundant, both you *and* I can have what we want.

### *Summary*

- The Principle of Abundance is the keystone of resolutionary thinking.
- There is no limit to what creativity can produce.
- We can apply the same principles of unlimited creativity to solving problems and resolving conflict as we do to new ventures.

### *Reflections*

- As you look at the remaining nine principles and review all of the case studies and examples, look for the perspective of abundance.
- Notice the situations in your life in which you were conditioned by a perspective of abundance. Did that perspective contribute to the outcome you wanted?
- Think of a current situation where you have not been getting the result you want. Imagine you have all the resources to get the outcome you desire. Is that approach helpful?

# 6

**PRINCIPLE 2**
## Creating Partnership

| OLD THINKING | NEW THINKING |
|---|---|
| *Wasting resources* | *Creating partnership* |

A man who dares to waste one hour has not discovered the value of life.

*Darwin*

People who are working together often waste resources because they do not have a clearly articulated vision of where they are going and how they will get there. They waste more resources resolving the inevitable conflicts that surface.

That was my belief when I started practicing law 37 years ago. It hasn't changed. This is true for all types of collaborations—business partnerships, joint ventures, intracompany teams, and employee/manager and professional/

client relationships. It's especially true for lovers and spouses. I think the waste is increasing as I look at the contentiousness and litigiousness in our daily headlines.

At the beginning, when you are very excited about the new venture or relationship, our traditional way of doing things asks you to focus on all the things that can go wrong. Once you scare yourself by thinking about all the what-ifs ("what if this . . . ," "what if that . . . "), your lawyer may do his or her best to "protect" you from any nasty things your new partner might do to you. This has the predictable effect of creating an adversary relationship before you begin working together. This can shift hopeful, positive expectations into distrust and polarization. It can get people so turned off that a well-intentioned collaboration never happens. You don't even have a honeymoon with your new collaborator, let alone time to enjoy it. It's not my intention to blame lawyers; they're doing the best they have been trained to do.

The inefficiency gets worse. If you find yourself in a disagreement you can't easily resolve, you may end up looking for truth and justice in a courtroom. That will cost you in many ways. You find yourself not communicating with a partner or spouse, not taking care of the real business of your life, and wasting more resources. In Chapter 2 we noted that the waste of resources includes direct cost, opportunity cost, continuity cost, and emotional cost.

The two brothers in Chapter 3 were on the road to wasting resources. If they had not taken the tack of resolutionary thinking, they would have followed the advice of their well-meaning lawyers, who were doing the best they knew how. The brothers may have wasted a few years trying to gain a strategic advantage within a context of traditional litigation. They would have suffered the waste of losing what they expected their business to produce and the diminished value of the business; the waste of the direct cost of two sets of lawyers and forensic experts;

the waste of what they might have produced if their attention was focused on productivity; the waste of losing the community they had built; the waste of the emotional resources drained by the conflict; and the loss of a brother.

Let's compare this to what actually happened. Within a short period of time they came together and efficiently resolved a difficult situation. Each moved on with his own life, expending minimal expenses, minimal time, and minimal emotional energy.

## Creating Agreements Efficiently

The adversarial mind-set pervades our thinking in many collaborative situations. We overlook the value of doing our best to make sure the partnership will be effective. The process of putting an effective agreement in place requires addressing many specific aspects of what you will do together, including acknowledging that conflict will occur and mapping out a strategy for dealing with it. Conflict prevention happens when you agree on how you will agree and how you will disagree, both of which are inevitable in a working relationship.

Efficiently detailing your new agreement at the beginning of a relationship, or when inevitable conflict occurs, has extraordinary value. Inefficiency often comes from not knowing what goes into a good agreement. Having a template for an agreement creates efficiency. You do not have to reinvent the wheel each time. You know the elements that have to be discussed, and you talk about them. If everyone can get on the same page at the beginning, time is not wasted with fits and starts about who will do what. A full and complete conversation at the beginning enables you to decide efficiently if it is appropriate to move forward. This prevents wasting resources on a doomed transaction.

When I first developed the agreement template that is discussed in Chapter 20, I felt like a kid with a new toy. I was thrilled by the surprised reaction people had when I would ask a few questions of each person in a collaboration and the next day produce an agreement that satisfied everyone. It expressed the participants' vision of what they wanted to happen, not how they would be protected if things go wrong.

## Creating an Efficient Collaboration

Getting a successful project up and running is an exercise in forming a collaborative team. It requires going through some conflict, but not as much as traditional wisdom would have you believe. Teams go through four stages: forming, storming, norming, and performing.[10] The conflict involved in passing through these stages cannot be avoided, but it can be minimized if (1) a team agreement is put in place at the beginning, and (2) everyone is willing to use the principles and model presented in this book and quickly engage in conversations for resolution when conflict arises. I continue to be excited when I work with start-up organizations who have made a commitment to building an organizational culture based on clear, explicit agreements. Their excitement is infectious as they see how simple what they struggled with can be.

I used to withdraw quickly from projects that were diverting time and energy from a declared mission. I noticed that members of the team were more concerned with personal power and individual success than with accomplishing stated objectives. I have learned that if you can stay focused on agreed-upon goals and objectives while operating from shared vision and values, all else will fall into place. The challenge: learning to let go of ego concerns. A key is to embrace a mindset of abundance—everyone can win without the need for a loser. Keeping our eyes on the big picture, seeing the forest through the trees, and losing certain battles for the sake of the larger cause are clichés, but they emphasize that continuing is usually more efficient than leaving, despite the temporary conflict. Starting over is usually very inefficient.

If efficient front-end agreements and resolution processes are created at the beginning of a project, they will keep a team focused on goals. Although you never know what will happen on a journey, it is better not to begin unless you can maximize your chances for success.

## *Summary*

- Present day standard practice wastes enormous amounts of resources in both reaching agreement and resolving conflict.

- Conserving human and material resources is accomplished by having efficient agreement and resolution processes.

## *Reflections*

- Think of a situation in which you need to create clear agreements with a collaborator.

- Use the ten-element agreement model in Chapter 20 to form your collaboration.

- Does the clearly expressed vision in the explicit agreement help?

# 7

# Being Creative

| OLD THINKING | NEW THINKING |
|---|---|
| *Problem, issue, emotion* | *Being creative* |

Imagination is more important than knowledge.

*Albert Einstein*

Most people are emotionally upset when facing differences and conflict. They are frustrated because they have adopted the prevailing attitude that all things should unfold as "I" see them and should be perfect, smooth, and without rough edges. Shouldn't they? Aren't we entitled to be upset when they aren't?

## Conflict as an Ordinary and Expected Phenomenon

When I listen to businesspeople and lawyers talk, it is often about the issues that upset, concern, or worry them. Many people have difficulty accepting that life is filled with surprises, conflict, disappointment, unmet expectations, and change. These things happen, consistently and predictably. This phenomenon was elegantly expressed by an infant I recently saw at the airport. Mom was preparing the child for a feeding, and she pulled out a beautiful embroidered bib. Across the infant's chest it read:

## Spit Happens

Yes, spit happens! What you do with it, how you deal with it, your attitude toward it—that marks the quality of your life.

Have you ever been in a recurrent conflict with a family member or colleague? Each time the conflict jumps out at you, it is impossible to think about a creative solution. You are gripped by your own emotion, and from within this strong reaction there is little possibility of creativity.

One of my college roommates never cleaned his room. I could not think about creative resolutions because, when I saw the clutter, I had strong emotional reactions. A few years later I was confronted with a similar situation. By then, I had trained myself to say STOP! as I observed myself moving into a strong emotional reaction of judgment. Stopping enables me to respond with the focus on a creative solution before the trigger is pulled and the emotion explodes, rendering me useless.

There is no return on investing unnecessary emotional energy. We do not have unlimited capacity, and when we hold onto the emotion we are harming ourselves physically, given that stress is the greatest cause of disease. As my partner Irving used to say, "Stewart, you cannot un-punch someone!"

Learning to treat conflict as ordinary and expected is the goal. When you learn that, you can focus your resources on creative solutions.

## Creativity in Action

Observing how we talk to ourselves is both the fundamental element of emotional intelligence,[11] and a key part of learning to live in the principle of creativity. It is useful to program yourself not to use the word *problem* when confronted by any situation that has potential for conflict. One option is reframing the situation as an opportunity to demonstrate your creativity. Before your emotions render you useless, think about what would be the most effective action. When someone tells you there is a problem to deal with, just smile and say, "Here is an opportunity to demonstrate how creative we can be." The key is how we talk to ourselves. If we want to see the glass as half full, then our internal conversation must say that the situation is an opportunity and not a problem.

Let's look at two examples of creativity in action.

### *Broaden Your Perspective*

Both of the brothers in Chapter 3 were following a traditional route. The lawyers they consulted saw this as a series of legal issues to be resolved: Who had more voting stock in the corporation? Who was violating his obligations to the organization? Was anyone abandoning his responsibilities? Was anyone wasting the assets of the organization? Is there any entitlement to a payout? What is the value of the business? Dealing with those mixed legal and business valuation issues is enough to keep a small army of lawyers and forensic accountants busy for a while. No one was looking at the situation from the practical perspective of dealing creatively with a going concern in a way that would preserve value.

I had no bias about what was supposed to happen. There was no restriction limiting my thinking about a potential outcome. The major focus was coming up with a resolution that honored the concerns expressed by the brothers.

Even though there might be fighting, you don't have to see it as a fight; even though there is willfulness, you don't have to see the situation as a test of wills; even though there are legal issues, you don't have to see the situation as a legal battle; even though there are accounting issues, you don't have to see it as an accounting problem.

With resolutionary thinking, the conflict is seen as an exercise in creative problem solving. That led the two brothers beyond the value judgments that create issues, problems, and emotions. It coaxed them to the terrain of creativity. They came up with the solution because they followed the mindset of collaboration. We arrived at a landscape no expert had explored because it was not within the discipline of their profession.

### An Organic Agreement

**Selena and Sergio.** Selena and Sergio came from traditional backgrounds. It was agreed that Selena would teach school and put Sergio through graduate school. To an observer it looked like a very conservative union. Aside from their marriage vows, they had only one explicit agreement: They agreed to stay together as long as it remained fun.

Their marriage thrived for ten years. They were fulfilled and prosperous, and they had a wonderful home and many friends. After ten years each caught a dose of wanderlust. There was more angst and confinement than the fun they had agreed to. They decided to separate. They allowed their relationship, and the agreement that contained it, to grow—no lawyers, no high drama, no bitterness. They remain the best of friends, being there for each other as the need arose.

They have allowed their friendship to develop creatively, based on their personal needs. Rather than act on their knee-jerk judgments and evaluations of each other, they have chosen to honor the profound respect each has for the other's personal process. Neither one knows where the connection will lead. The only certainty is that they stay in touch as they ride the waves of change and transition in their respective lives. Rather than referencing what goes on between them against an external standard of what is "supposed" to be, they allow themselves the freedom to create in uncharted waters.

Trusting yourself enough to paint on a blank canvas is the essence of creativity. It can lead to results that are way beyond traditional expectations. Shifting our patterns of thinking is not a simple activity that yields immediate results. It takes intention and commitment. When people ask how to cross the barrier I must admit there is no magic pill—it takes self awareness and perseverance in believing you are on the way to a better result. A useful game is to catch yourself in old thinking patterns and remind yourself why you want to make changes, and what you see as a more effective outcome. Remember the cost of conflict. Another recently articulated and very powerful perspective is the role personal identity and emotional development plays in the way we chose to hold onto our own perspective. Letting go might be much easier if we had insight and awareness that what we may be holding onto is nothing less than a part of our personal identity.[12]

## Summary

- Most professionals and businesspeople are conditioned to think of issues and problems framed in terms of their own domain of expertise

- Experts fix problems according to their professional standards of right/wrong

- Most people have a belief system that says conflict and disagreement are bad.

- When you combine the restrictive approach of being self-referential and needing to fix with the fear of consequences of conflict, the chance of getting stuck multiplies.

- Moving to a broader field of creativity enhances the potential for satisfactory resolution because it removes the constraints and broadens the field of potential solutions.

## Reflections

- Think of a few situations of conflict in your life that were resolved to your satisfaction. Were you limited by beliefs about what you thought proper, right, or wrong?

- Think of some current conflicts. What potential creative resolutions do you see when you remove the limitations of your own thinking?

# 8

**PRINCIPLE 4**
# Fostering Sustainable Collaboration

| OLD THINKING | NEW THINKING |
|---|---|
| *Fostering conflict* | *Fostering sustainable collaboration* |

If you do not wish to be prone to anger, do not feed the habit; give it nothing which may tend to its increase. At first, keep quiet and count the days when you were not angry: "I used to be angry every day, then every other day: next, every two, then every three days!" and if you succeed in passing thirty days, sacrifice to the gods in thanksgiving.

*Epictetus*

Traditional systems and ways of thinking about conflict resolution are often akin to spraying gasoline on a fire. The flames get hotter and higher. Although there are situations in which the teeth of our administrative and legal systems are essential (see Chapter 24), many standard interventions like grievances, complaints, hearings, suits, countersuits, motions, depositions, and interrogatories are "courtly" games few can afford to play.

The following things often happen when you get involved with standard methods for resolving conflict:

1. Your lawyer does the "lawyering"—filing lawsuits and the like.

2. Your conflict is classified to fit within a legal theory, deflecting the inquiry from the underlying personal conflict.

3. Your lawyer will likely instruct you to stop talking to the other people involved.

4. The goal becomes winning, not resolution or preserving the relationship.

5. Little is done to address your emotional pain and your grief over the lost expectation you anticipated in the transaction or relationship.

6. The standard practice of professional hourly billing is an inherent conflict of interest that does not motivate resolution.

7. Your conflict becomes your advocate's case. Ego and greed may take the conflict to places other than resolution.

8. The process wears you down. The technical rules of the legal game may keep out the most important information and prevent an authentic exploration.

9. It may take years to get before a judge. When you finally get there, the judge wants you to settle because judges prefer matters that focus on novel issues or impact many people. Or, you may get a judge who is not very smart!

10. Finding truth is often elusive. Justice can be a roll of the dice, not found in formal proceedings.

11. Getting the case "settled" is more important than the quality of the resolution—resolving the real concerns.

Except in narrow circumstances all of these aspects of the current systems for resolving conflict can and usually do make the conflict worse.

## Fostering Resolution with Collaboration

In a resolutionary mode of thinking, reaching agreements and addressing differences take place within a context of resolution. Creative, collaborative systems for making agreements and resolving conflicts are the norm. Reaching agreement is no longer an adversarial negotiation. Negotiating becomes about creating a composite, shared vision of the desired outcome. Built into the agreement is the understanding that disagreement will happen. Dealing with disagreements is framed as an opportunity to deepen the agreement, not a feared breakdown. All are inside the same circle, standing together, shoulder to shoulder, wondering how best to take care of their shared concerns while envisioning together the future they want to create.

The two brothers followed the paradigm of fostering resolution. It was opposite from the path their lawyers selected. They had both been told to stop communicating—that the path to resolution was a court battle. This made it much worse than it had to be.

Instead, the brothers used a process designed to diffuse conflict and move quickly to resolution. Each told his story and then listened to the other's story, so each brother would know what was happening in the other's mind. This provided venting and catharsis. Next, they went through a "completion" process: all that needed to be said to get to the core of the conflict was voiced. That facilitated their grieving the loss of their expectations for the family business. Then they could move forward. Getting every aspect of the conflict in the open is essential. But if they had not talked to each other, nothing would be left of their business. That does not foster resolution.

Recently a friend referred a new client. My friend was a "reformed sinner." He had approached me a year ago about a litigation in which he was involved. Unfortunately it was too late in what was a very costly learning experience for him. He asked me "What can I do to prevent that from ever happening again?" As a result of some coaching on my part and learning on his part he now understands the lessons of this chapter. When he was told of the situation within my new client's family, they were on the path of lawyers and legal intervention. My resolutionary thinking mind-set suggested to him that a simple but emotional conversation with her husband would be the best place for his client to begin. That's what she did. So with 15 minutes of resolutionary thinking she spared herself a great deal of time, energy, emotion, and money.

Many lawyers make a great living within the systems for resolving conflict. Sometimes they provide an invaluable service. But in most situations there is a better way. Whenever a new judge is appointed, I say to myself, "Four mediators would foster much more resolution." Fortunately, mine is not the only voice speaking for reform.

### Summary

- Current standard practice often makes things worse by fanning the fires of conflict.

- It is critically important to take steps that dissipate the conflict and move to resolution before making things worse in the name of standard practice.

## Reflections

- If you have ever been involved in litigation, spend ten minutes writing about what the process was like and your emotions as you were in it.

- If you have not been involved in litigation, find someone who has and interview them about what the process was like. Ask how litigation affected the conflict in terms of intensity, duration, levels of trust, ability to work together, and emotional release.

- Ask if the person was satisfied with the result and whether the situation was resolved.

- Think of some current conflicts. What steps might you take that would foster resolution? By when will you take action?

# 9

## PRINCIPLE 5
# Becoming Open

| OLD THINKING | NEW THINKING |
| --- | --- |
| *Righteous bravado and posturing* | *Becoming open* |

Show Up.
Pay Attention.
Tell Your Truth.
Don't Be Attached to the Outcome.

Angelis Arrien, PhD, *The Four Fold Way*[13]

Under the accepted paradigm, people in conflict posture. They play games. They horse around. The focus is more about being right than being effective. Winning has become the highest value. No one gets points for candor!

Many of our role models come from television. *Dallas, L.A. Law, Perry Mason, Boston Legal, Ali McBeal, Eli Stone, Shark, Law & Order,* and the O.J. Simpson trials are examples.

The bravado we see, and often follow, seems cool as a sound bite, but it doesn't get us the results we want. Saying "I'll see you in court" may feel great in the moment because we see the hero do it on TV, but it can be like going down the rabbit hole with Alice. We may do something in the moment to save face, be cool, or act macho in an uncomfortable situation. We want to make sure we look good. Often we end up in a more difficult place because of what we have done in the name of our bravado. A few years ago I was interviewed for an article in *Written By*, the trade magazine of the Writers Guild of America.[14] The interviewer said that most screenplays follow the formula of "conflict, high drama, violence, resolution."

The question for me was whether you could cut out the violence and maintain the high drama necessary for a great screenplay. Of course I said yes, immediately thinking of the many amazing and poignant moments of high drama present in some of the resolutions I have been part of.

## Reprogramming Yourself to Be Open

People often act from bravado because they have never seen another way. Soft-spoken openness, vulnerability, and the honesty and self-disclosure attached to it, do not usually sell movies, books, or TV shows. There are few visible role models for this behavior. And yet, in my workshops around the country, the qualities that audiences consistently mention as admirable are honesty, listening, authenticity, lack of ego, and understanding another perspective.

Because of the cultural pressures to be otherwise, being vulnerable and open is not often honored and rewarded. But openness and authenticity is an easy, natural way to be. Being open is not being weak. Being open is being your real, authentic self. Getting beyond your initial resistance is challenging, but once beyond that resistance, it is the easiest behavior to adopt.

What I mean by openness and vulnerability is summed up at the beginning of this chapter by Angelis Arrien as the four guides for all human interaction. You are fully present, without an act, story, or angle. You tell *your* truth without the need to have the outcome be a certain way. That is a great way to stay centered and empty of the kind of emotional attachment that will get you in trouble. There is no acting or scheming; you are simply yourself. It's easy because you don't worry about being consistent with your previous "act" or story; you don't have to second-guess yourself, or posture. You just show up and tell your truth.

The two brothers did not initially come to the table in an open place of vulnerability. The questions and inquiry of the resolution process took them to a place of openness and vulnerability they did not expect to go. I knew that to achieve resolution it was essential to tap into emotional areas of vulnerability surrounding their relationship as brothers. It is a commonly understood psychological phenomenon that before you can move through an emotional trauma, you must grieve the loss. But the grieving can't happen unless you go to a place of vulnerability with yourself and others. Proceeding traditionally never gets you to vulnerability because it requires bravado and posturing. The brothers started on that path because they thought it was their only option. They found a better way.

## Opening to Vulnerability

*Maria and Scott.* Maria and Scott were convinced that after years of searching they had found the mates who would fulfill their dreams. They constructed an explicit agreement for all areas of their life, personal and professional. This detailed document put into words their vision for their future.

The unique feature of the agreement was the absence of an "out" clause. Because each had suffered the pain of failed relationships, they wanted to minimize that risk. But in the midst of the passion, promise, and expectation, they had created a contractual marriage. These two free spirits designed a prison for themselves. Because of their integrity and the strength of their commitment, they tried to live within their agreement. But, despite best intentions, they were having a very difficult time, made more so by their also being business partners.

They opened to the deepest levels of vulnerability as they worked with therapists, counselors, consultants and other well-meaning professionals to find a way to make their relationship functional. After five years they decided to renegotiate their agreement, despite their written-in-stone promises. They agreed to separate their professional and personal lives. Letting go was as painful as coming together had been joyful. They learned the wisdom of the organic quality of any relationship. They have no unfinished business or emotional baggage. Their vulnerability left nothing unsaid.

Because of our culture's prevalent role models, it will take generations to shift our attitudes about humility and vulnerability. People are not used to being open with each other. Looking good and using sound bites are empty substitutes for sharing authenticity and personal truth. The following process is an excellent vehicle for helping people open to their vulnerability.

## The Truth Circle

The Truth Circle is a process that generates honest communication, a key ingredient of vulnerability. It is very effective in building work teams and with families. It uses a talking stick, an object that confers on the holder the right to talk while everyone listens. A group sits in a circle and chooses a topic for speaking the truth. The talking stick is passed around three times. At first people are uncomfortable, but as they warm to the process their truth emerges. It is a great way to invite people into an experience of vulnerability. We need the practice, because given our cultural conditioning, being vulnerable is counterintuitive.

## *Summary*

- Posturing and righteous bravado do not support resolution. They distance you from real concerns that need addressing.
- You have been programmed by cultural role models.
- You must learn, through practice, the power and simplicity of authentic vulnerability.

## *Reflections*

- Think about a time when you were posturing. Did it help you resolve the situation?
- If you had been forthcoming, would the situation have ended differently? Would the result have been more to your liking?
- Is there a current situation in which you could show more openness and vulnerability? What can you say or do? When will you take action?

# 10

## Forming
## Long-Term
## Collaborations

| OLD THINKING | NEW THINKING |
|---|---|
| *Short-term Adversary* | *Long-term Collaborations* |

The man who gets the most satisfactory results is not always the man with the most brilliant single mind, but rather the man who can best co-ordinate the brains and talents of his associates.

*W. Alton Jones*

We are often conditioned to think in terms of a short-term horizon, an immediate victory. We see only this quarter's bottom line, not this year's—let alone next year's or the next decade's.

Unfortunately, fear is often what drives us in the short term. Often it is fear of failure. If fear is your prevalent emotional state, any situation can become adversarial. Fear precludes trust and, when we fear, other people become adversaries we want to control and conquer. They become the enemy. The saddest aspect of this phenomenon is that it often automatically, unconsciously operates between people who want to collaborate.

## The "Now" Culture

We come by our short-term, adversarial mindset honestly. We have been influenced by an era of what I call "Lone-Rangerism"—solo-riding, conquer-the-west, rugged-individual, Marlboro-man, immediate-gratification, this-quarter, me-generation thinking! No wonder the notion of teams, collaboration, virtual organizations, and win/win outcomes are creating havoc in many organizations. We are asking for vast changes in the way people view others, while our personal programming and organizational metrics are driving us to be top-gun, king-of-the-hill, victorious individuals—**now**! The skill and patience it takes to work with others is what we really need, but it's not part of the way we have been conditioned.

Winning is deeply embedded in our national psyche. The word *win* is synonymous with success. Unfortunately, it also implies the corresponding *lose*. Even though the term *win/win* is used in many places, most of us think "for me to win, you must lose." Though win/win is pervasive in organizations, the idea of everyone winning is not yet an operational principle people fully embrace. (Win/win is OK, just as long as I win a little more!) Though we say the words, we do not believe or fully understand them. This is a great source of inner conflict, and the paradox and confusion pulls people in opposite directions and gives them a headache!

## The New Culture of Collaboration

I see the new way of working as a vision of two people standing shoulder to shoulder, viewing a situation of potential conflict. Under old thinking people are squared off, face to face, confronting each other. In the new paradigm they are looking at the situation together, envisioning a solution that will meet the challenge. They think of themselves as collaborators, co-creators, jointly designing the most favorable outcome. They remain in a relationship, building and deepening trust as their developing collaboration is forged and tempered by the challenges of conflict and differences.

Both know that, no matter what, from a broad perspective, they want the same outcome—a successful venture or relationship with a conflict resolution process that is respectful. They look together for the vessel that is large enough to hold and satisfy all the concerns that each of them has in the situation. They approach tasks, no matter how difficult, with a minimum of angst and emotion, and with the elegance of knowing that they will honor the challenge by caring about the long-term impact on all stakeholders, including themselves. Long-term impact is key. Whatever the situation, they do not see their relationship as a short-term, one-shot deal. They view situations with a longer horizon. Let's look at long-term collaboration within several circumstances.

## The Legal Community

After practicing law with the New Jersey attorney general's office, I joined a law firm in a small New Jersey town. This was in the early 1970s, just before the population of lawyers exploded. I had to accept that the lawyer who was on the opposite side of a case today might be on my side in the future. Since the legal community was small, taking a short-term perspective would come around to bite me. This encouraged civility. A few years later I moved to Manhattan. Because the population of lawyers was so large, most lawyers had a short-term perspective.

They assumed they would never deal with you again. I resisted making the adjustment because it meant that no one could be trusted.

A short-term perspective violates standards of ethics and fair play. Feeling good about yourself, which impacts your health and well-being, requires a longer view. In terms of your relationship to yourself, you're in it for the long haul. As Jon Kabat-Zinn says, "Wherever you go, there you are."[15] Taking the long view requires adopting the mind-set that you will be working with this person in the future. Make believe that you live in the same small town. More and more, as a result of technology, you do; it's called a global village. Make sure you won't feel compelled to cross the street out of embarrassment when someone is walking toward you, or when you run into them in the supermarket or at a PTA meeting.

## Teammates

*Raj and Ted.* The aerospace plant where Raj and Ted were engineers was being reorganized into a collaborative team environment. They had known each other for about three years. They never exchanged more than a nod because they had a strong negative reaction to each other. Neither of them knew why, but they knew the dislike was mutual. Now they were on the same team, required to work together.

For six weeks they skirted the tension as the team organized. Then they were on the same project, asked to produce designs jointly for a key engine component. They both complained to their wives and to the team coach. Their wives just listened. The coach said that learning how to work together was part of learning how to be a good team player, especially if you don't like a teammate. That did not make them feel any better or resolve their struggle.

As Ted and Raj observed each other while working together, slowly at first, but with gathering momentum, respect grew. They began to acknowledge each other's competence. As they became more comfortable, they found shared common interests, including a similar sense of humor. They became the backbone of their team, guiding others to greater levels of productivity and satisfaction.

As engineers, Ted and Raj observed how repulsion transformed into attraction. They said it was about going beyond their emotional reaction to a place of deeper understanding. They came to this because: (1) they had no choice about working together, (2) their coach suggested they observe and reserve their judgments and emotional reactions, and (3) they had to think of a long-term horizon.

## The Marriage Contract

*Lee and Kyung.* After a traditional courtship, Lee decided he wanted to marry Kyung. Although she loved him, Kyung was reluctant to marry. She had had a very unstable childhood. Because of her background, a condition of her marrying Lee was that they not have children. This was her bottom-line position: end of story, no discussion, issue closed. Lee agreed, and they were married.

Seven years later, Lee, with more than a little apprehension about approaching his wife, decided he wanted kids. Lee asked Kyung to take another look at the decision she made seven years earlier. He was smart in the way he framed the situation. He didn't make Kyung wrong about the decision she had made. He didn't make a demand. Lee asked her to revisit the choice after acknowledging that the choice she had made seven years ago was the best choice for her at the time.

Instead of digging in her heels, calling her lawyer, or just saying no, Kyung agreed to reconsider. This was not easy, given her history, but there had been many changes in her life. Kyung and Lee had both established professional careers. As a result, Kyung had a strong inner foundation, something she did not have as a child. Even if the marriage failed, she knew she could sustain herself and her children. The circumstance in which she had grown up no longer existed. The reason not to have children was no longer a concern. Rather than hold onto her position, Kyung was willing to revisit the choice she had made.

Twenty-five years later, Kyung is very pleased with her change of heart. Although the marriage ended, her children are the joy of her life. She is happy with the new choice she made.

The best agreements are organic. They grow over the long term.

## Friendship

Friendship is a classic example of the principle of "long-term-ness." All valuable relationships go through cycles. A friend once said "I really admire long-distance runners." She was commenting on the ability to ride out the rough spots of disagreement that inevitably arise in friendships. It's part of the process when you have a long-term horizon.

It would be easier if we could transcend our emotions as we go through disagreements. But if you have experienced the joy of long-term associations, you know that in the long run the upheavals look small compared to the richness that friendship brings.

## A Longer-Term Perspective

Our travel and mobility as a culture contributes to our anxiety and feelings of aloneness. A sense of separateness perpetuates the ease with which we blow others off. When we lived in smaller villages, we had to go through the conflict and come out the other side. There was no place to run. I think it's important to put back in place the context of having to live with people for the long term. We must live with our own response to the way we interact with others.

In the two brothers' situation, the longer-term perspective of "brothers for life" was voiced. Although they did not fully buy into it at first, they understood it was important. As the process unfolded, they came to appreciate the longer-term perspective. Because there is little concern for consequences when a short-term perspective is operative, things are skewed. A sense of continuity makes most people feel good. Richness, depth, and the ability to produce long-term results come from associations that go through cycles. It is important for people to reflect on this when experiencing short-term difficulty. That perspective helps us get what we really want—sustained long-term relationships.

### *Summary*

- You can choose to operate from a short-term or a long-term perspective.

- If you think and act as if a collaboration will be long-term, you will feel good about the relationship and yourself.

- You never know when the relationship will take on long-term significance, or when you will have to face the other person in your neighborhood. Remember—we all live in a global village!

### Reflections

- Think about a situation in which you either were taken advantage of or took advantage of someone for a short-term gain.

- How did it feel? What emotions are generated by the situation?

- How would you act differently if you could do it over? How might you act in a similar situation in the future that would reflect a long term perspective?

# 11

## PRINCIPLE 7
# Relying on Feelings and Intuition

| OLD THINKING | NEW THINKING |
|---|---|
| *Logical* | *Relying on feelings and intuition* |

When dealing with people, remember you are not dealing with creatures of logic, but with creatures of emotion, creatures bristling with prejudice and motivated by pride and vanity.

*Dale Carnegie*

Although attitudes are changing, most people still accept that the world operates on the premise of logic. Aristotle and Newton would be proud of how we follow their basic cognitive precepts about the way the world works. Everything fits into a category, A flows into B, and consequences are predictable.

## Beyond the Five Senses

Based on what is being written and what traditional institutions are integrating (alternative and Eastern forms of medicine are good examples), I believe we may be on the verge of creating a new foundation. The scientific method needs to be supplemented. In this global village, we are facing many challenges so complex that new theoretical models are needed for the solutions and resolutions to our current challenges.

A wonderful example of this kind of inquiry is the bestseller *Leadership and the New Science* by Margaret Wheatley, a businessperson, consultant, and professor.[16] Wheatley noticed that most of the fundamental principles around which we build organizations and institutions are grounded in Newtonian logic. This conceptualizes the world in terms of "materialism and reductionism—a focus on things other than relationships." Newtonian logic was leading-edge thinking at the time his fundamental principles were adopted. As I write, a dialogue is taking place about the benefit social and value networks add to an organization as well as Ken Wilbur's *A Brief History of Everything* and Eckart Tolle's *The Power of Now*.[17]

To see what was at the leading edge of thinking, Margaret Wheatley decided to explore current scientific developments in various disciplines. She found that, in all the natural sciences, currently accepted paradigms had gone way beyond Newton. The foundational assumptions on which we built our institutions and organizations have been transcended; in fact, chaos is often the operative principle. Our organizational theory has always been firmly grounded in scientific principles; perhaps it's time to update the theory to align with current scientific thinking.

In the old ways of scientific thinking, we looked at evidence in terms of the five physical senses—sight, sound, touch, smell, and taste. Today we know there is much more. We can take into consideration feeling, emotion, and intuition as well as logic.

This change is illustrated by various police departments' use of psychics to help solve major crimes or find missing people. The much-discussed use of astrologers in the White House—not to mention a consultation with Jean Houston, the noted New Age guru—are good examples of new thinking. A professional mediation journal recently featured an article that compared the metaphor of mediator as "trickster" to the generally accepted notion of mediator as a "professional" who consistently follows accepted operating theories. Trickster was not meant in a derogatory way, but in the Native American sense to indicate a wider range of options.[18] And, the Harvard Law School *Negotiation Journal* published an excellent scholarly article about mediation and meditation![19]

In domains previously thought to be grounded only in the world of logic, we are now allowing a broader spectrum of our "human-beingness" to be recognized as operative and important. This applies to resolving conflict in two important ways:

1. We can rely on feelings and intuition in getting to resolution.

2. We can use feelings and intuition as a factor for determining that resolution has been reached.

I remember feeling blasphemous when I started telling my legal clients that their written agreements were not as important as their feelings of whether they could trust another person. Even though my profession is steeped in written tradition, to me trust was much more important than a tightly drafted contract. In the Model of Resolution introduced in Part IV, I discuss the "phenomenon" of agreement. This is a heartfelt assessment of whether agreement exists after two or more people engage in the process of discussing essential elements that make up their agreement. You can say all the right words, it can look tidy, and you may still not have an agreement because something is missing at a gut level. There is no covenant.

When I work with intimate personal relationships—executives, partners, family businesses, divorces—I will not address financial and property issues until clients complete the conflict resolution model, a process designed to have them confront the difficult emotional aspects of the breakdowns in their working relationships. I know that the emotional pain is the real cause of the difficulty. Until you grieve, you cannot get beyond the conflict. When starting out on a new venture, one of the most important disclosures is "fears or concerns" about the transaction. Surfacing those emotions and addressing them are keys to crafting a covenant, an agreement that will last.

In the two brothers' situation, emotions were highly charged. Unless emotional release was provided, no effective resolution was possible. Instead, as often happens, people continue to act out their unconscious reactions and unexpressed emotions. We must learn to acknowledge the presence of these strong emotions and provide the place for them to surface. Absent venting, resolution will never happen.

*Carol and Steven.* Carol and Steven were trusting partners, joyous about the prospect of working together. They had "grown up" as professional trainers for the same Silicon Valley high-tech company. They admired and respected each other. Each had run their own business for about four years. Both were tired of working alone. When they ran into each other at an association meeting, they had a long conversation. They talked about the challenges of working alone and the responsibility of carrying the entire show on one set of shoulders. They were doing the same things—custom-designed training for new subscribers of specialized management software. If they joined forces, the economies of scale would be substantial.

Quickly, and with a great deal of exuberance, they decided to be partners. The partnership agreement consisted of a handshake and an agreement to work out all the details as they came up. Through ups and downs, arguments and admiration, they have learned to work things out by listening and accepting different approaches. The partnership has thrived for five years, without any formal explicit agreement. Carol and Steve attribute their success to the respect, trust, and thankfulness they have for their work and to the pleasure and joy of the collaboration.

They relish the creativity and excitement of painting on a blank canvas each time they make decisions. It has been suggested that they craft a formal partnership agreement. To date they have declined. They resist because things are working so well. The artist in me understands. When something is working well and feels right, leave it alone—just enjoy it!

I think we are all emotional creatures. I no longer believe people who say they can be objective. We are all subjective! The challenge is knowing what our bias is so we can factor it into the equation.

### Summary

- When dealing with people, you must factor in emotions because they are present in all situations.

- In more and more arenas, the nonlinear, nonrational is accepted.

## Reflections

- Examine the areas of your life that are not run by pure logic and rational analysis.

- Are these nonlinear perceptual systems valuable for you?

- In what ways are they a contribution?

# 12

PRINCIPLE 8
## Disclosing
## Information
## and Feelings

| OLD THINKING | NEW THINKING |
|---|---|
| *Hoarding and controlling information* | *Disclosing information and feelings* |

> If there is nothing worthwhile to hide, then secrecy will earn the appropriate mistrust without providing any benefits.
>
> *Edward DeBono* [20]

Information is king. Whoever has it can hoard, use, and manipulate it. Nondisclosure—providing limited access and cutting off communication—is an accepted way of conducting business. But this game of nondisclosure dilutes the ability to get to resolution.

## The Raw Material for Resolution

When disagreement erupts, often the flow of information halts. People stop talking. Documents are not shared until required. This is unfortunate. Conflict and disagreement are the clearest signs that more, not less, information needs to be exchanged. Information and discussion, with facts and ideas shared, are the raw material from which resolution emerges. Cutting the flow ensures conflict, delay, and lack of consensus about the outcome.

A rich parallel comes from the business community. Traditionally, management has held onto information—strategic, competitive, and, especially, financial. A company called Springfield Remanufacturing once ran into severe trouble. The board decided to be candid with all of the company's employees. The board members told everyone their plight: if the company did not turn around, it was on a trajectory toward financial failure. The employees responded with resourcefulness. Their innovations not only kept the company from bankruptcy but they also turned the organization into a thriving, highly profitable business. The key was that management had to provide the information employees needed to solve existing problems. They called it "open-book" management.[21]

If you are joint venturers working on a new project with each having proprietary information, you may be hesitant to share information. But that will impede reaching the joint goal. For example, if you are different drug manufacturers working on a solution to cancer, hesitating to share what you already know will compromise the bigger goal: finding a cure. In the world of Wikinomics[22] you would readily share all the information you have. You may have to reach agreement first about allocating profit or prizes, but you understand that disclosure is essential for reaching your objective.

## Clearing the Highway

A colleague of mine was asked to make a last-ditch attempt to resolve a stalled highway project. It was part of the Interstate highway system started in the 1950s. The section in question was the north-south route through a major metropolitan center. The east-west route was up and running, as was the loop around the city, but the north-south route had stopped in the center of the city. The project started in 1957 and had been stalled since 1973. If my colleague was unsuccessful, the project would be scrapped. By the time he was consulted, an army of lawyers had created a morass of litigation, with enough documents to fill a courthouse. Stakeholders included:

The U.S. Government

The U.S. Department of Transportation

The U.S. Environmental Protection Agency

The U.S. Department of Energy

The state government

The state highway department

The state Environmental Protection Agency

Three county governments

Six municipal governments

A class representing 400 property owners

A homeowners' association

A historic preservation society

The Sierra Club

Nine contractors

Four municipal utilities

The level of hostility was high. Positions had been steeled by 20 years of impersonal litigation. In these situations, individuals lose their identity. They become faceless enemies with labels—plaintiffs, defendants, bleeding-heart environmentalists, heartless developers. This one even pitted advocates of state sovereignty against the federal authorities.

Imagine some of the costs of the conflict:

Direct costs of all the litigation—lawyers and experts

Lost productivity—time people spent in conflict

Extra time on the road for commuters and commercial vehicles

Opportunity cost of all those involved

Emotional cost

Loss of community

My colleague's first action was to set up a meeting with detailed ground rules for participation. A key ground rule was full disclosure of all that was going on—both what was being said and what was not being said. This meeting was to hear everyone's story—to allow them all to vent their current feelings, concerns, and what they hoped to achieve as an outcome.

The second meeting was to hear responses from each stakeholder to the concerns voiced by each of the other groups. This is called "walking in each other's shoes."

The third meeting asked stakeholders to role-play their "enemies." By now, the nameless and faceless parties were beginning to be seen as real people with legitimate interests and concerns.

Predictably, by the fourth meeting the desire to take care of other stakeholders started to emerge. This enabled consensus on all of the major issues. A feeling of joy started to emerge in the meeting room. They could finally return to the real business of their lives: the productivity of their own work and their personal sources of fulfillment.

In this case, full disclosure provided the grist for people to work with. Until everything is on the table, no one is dealing with the entire situation. The story also illustrates that resolution involves breaking an old habit: Instead of making sure your concerns are taken care of first, resolution incorporates the concerns of everyone. You must listen, understand, and honor others' concerns. Recognizing others' needs gets you what you want, and legitimizing others' concerns sets up the conditions in which others can take care of your concerns. That is an essential part of the foundation on which you construct resolution.

Once "their" concerns are seen as legitimate, they become your concerns too; because they are concerns of the situation, the solution will readily follow. This happens because you have people taking care of people, not people who have a position or people who want something. Taking care of others is natural for human beings.I believe a key reason situations resolve is the level of trust that develops when people are open and disclosing. This is also a critical determinant in whether people feel comfortable enough to continue working with each other.[23] I will say more about this in Chapter 20. I commend the work of two powerful books about trust. One is by Michelle and Dennis Reina and the other by Stephen Covey.[24] The roots of trust/no trust are imbedded deep in the biology of our primal brain. If our "system" says no there is a lot to overcome.

A key to resolving the brothers' situation was a frank discussion of what each wanted to do. Full disclosure is the keystone on which resolution is constructed. The steps of the model get people talking.

## Summary

- Information is the raw material that leads to resolution.
- Holding information can lead only to mistrust and escalation of conflict.
- Full disclosure is evidence of a good-faith effort to work together toward resolution.
- Full disclosure builds trust.

## Reflections

- Has secrecy and withholding information ever helped you get what you want for the long run?
- Think of a situation in which you are currently involved in which you have stopped communicating and sharing information. Begin communicating and sharing information. What happens?

# 13

**PRINCIPLE 9**
## Learning Throughout the Resolution Process

| OLD THINKING | NEW THINKING |
|---|---|
| *Winning, being right* | *Learning throughout the resolution process* |

> Do you have the patience to wait until your mud settles and the water is clear? Can you remain unmoving until the right action arises by itself?
>
> *Lao Tzu*

While focused on winning, you may not want to know or listen to the concerns of other people. Your objective is to convince everyone you are right, no matter what.

## Listening Leads to Learning

Assuming commitment and the necessary attitude of resolution, the process of coming together to resolve a conflict is an exercise in group learning. It's all about teaching and learning. Learning is a useful way to get rid of the ego-based ideas of winning, being right, fixing blame, or doing it the "right" way. Learning and being open to influence puts you in a mind-set of discovery, allowing you the luxury of not knowing the answers or the specific path that you will take. This process lets you discover, explore, and learn with everyone else what the best solution is. As the process unfolds, people are educating each other about their perception of the situation and simultaneously learning what is needed to understand the bigger picture.

Think of a group coming together with a set of desired outcomes. Everyone holds key information. No one knows the answer. By keeping the dialogue open the group arrives at an agreement in principle. For example, in a partnership dispute everyone wants a fair resolution so they can all get back to work. Through an open dialogue, during which you learn about the others' particular concerns, you learn your way to what an effective resolution might look like. The same is true for spouses, unhappy consumers, even strikers. The learning perspective is the most important component of creating value and opportunity in the situations that life presents. Resolutionaries don't know the answers, but they do know that the longer you can suspend knowing, the more comprehensive the learning, and the more creative the resolution will be. Until you know, you keep listening and learning.

Listening to others, and paying careful attention to your sensing systems, enables you to "learn your way through" without knowing what the outcome will be. Because of the trust it requires, I am honored whenever people grace me with the request to assist them. It is essential to learn to trust your responses. Don't look for the quick fix in situations where you are not clear, because you will only have to retrace your steps. Have the courage to stay with your uncertainty until the clouds disappear and clarity is revealed. To use the four-fold metaphor found at the beginning of Chapter 9, you must be present, listen to what is said, speak your truth, and allow yourself to be influenced by what you hear. That's what it means to be unattached to the outcome. You move off your position as a result of being educated by what others say.

In the two brothers' situation, no one knew what was going to happen. We educated each other in the process about needs and concerns. Eventually we all learned what we needed to design a satisfactory resolution. When you design a solution, it is important to check congruity with everyone as you go forward. The more the resolution incorporates the instruction of this feedback loop, the more satisfied everyone will be.

## The Learning Boss

Masoud had been the plant manager for 17 of the 34 years that he had worked for a famous appliance manufacturer. Although he was respected by everyone, he was one of those authoritarian micromanagers who told you what to do. "My way or the highway" expressed his management style. This served him well for many years, but the young managers reporting to him, who were responsible for operations, were from a new generation.

Alice, one of Masoud's managers, had her own thoughts about the crew she supervised. In the area of work hours, she wanted to accommodate the childcare concerns of both men and women. Masoud, however, believed the plant had three shifts, and that's when you punched your clock, period! Alice implemented some flexible scheduling for her workers. The productivity improvements were immediate and significant. Alice was accurate that concerns about children detracted from the focus and enthusiasm her workers brought to the job.

Masoud found out what was going on. He was not pleased with Alice or with her initiative. Oblivious to the results, he focused on the violation of "his" rules. He sent a memo to all supervisors outlining his policy, intimating that anyone violating the rule would be terminated. He did not mention Alice by name.

Alice persisted. Although she had the support of the vice president of human resources, she did not want to play this trump card. Alice felt the tension grow between her and Masoud. It robbed her of time and energy for other productivity improvements.

Alice decided to resolve the matter. She had several goals in mind: (1) to gain Masoud's approval of flex time, (2) to impress upon him the importance of listening to employees, and (3) to consider the unique situation everyone brings to the workplace. She asked to meet with Masoud.

With the skills of international diplomacy, tact and the experience of 30 years as a wife and mother of six, she asked Masoud to think back to the time when his family was young. She had him step into his wife's shoes. She asked him to imagine how his wife might be less than fully present on the job if she was concerned about the welfare of their children. Alice also had Masoud think about how he would react as a father if he shared the responsibility for childcare. Masoud started to see her point. She then pointed to the productivity increases. Reluctantly at first, but with growing enthusiasm, Masoud started to come around. Two critical factors enabled Alice to be successful in getting her boss to engage: (1) the diplomatic nature of her communication skills and (2) the business case she developed. Those two factors are always essential when dealing with unequal power relationships.

Masoud has become a plant hero. With Alice's help, he developed new work rules. Now employees create their own schedules. The productivity improvements and increased autonomy of plant workers have greatly impacted the way workers feel about their jobs. That translates into greater efficiency and reduced turnover and absenteeism. Reluctantly, Masoud gave himself permission to learn what contributed to his long-term effectiveness as a plant manager. If he had remained concerned about being right, he would have missed the lessons.

## The Circle of Partnership

*Carl and Mitchell.* Carl and Mitchell decided to leave the safety of the large law firm in which they were partners. One Saturday they sat at the same computer terminal and filled in the blanks of a boilerplate partnership agreement. They agreed to be the meanest lawyers their city had to offer.

They had both been through many battles about broken partnerships. They felt experienced enough to structure their own agreement. They addressed all of the legal details, including monthly draws and sharing income, professional incorporation, termination, and what would happen in the event of their death. They even agreed how to divide files if they split up. What never entered their mind was what would happen if they developed philosophical differences about their work.

About three years into the partnership, Carl had a serious family tragedy. His 7-year-old daughter was killed by a hit-and-run driver. Most people expected that the incident would harden him, but it had the opposite effect. Carl lapsed into a period of introspection and reflection. He interpreted the death as a signal, a punishment, a wake-up call. Carl was sure this was the payback for all the hard-nosed lawyering he had been doing in the name of professionalism and being the best, which for him meant being the toughest.

During this time of introspection, he explored the field of mediation. He realized that in many situations he had not been providing value for his clients. Carl decided that mediation was a better way of resolving conflict. He started recommending this route to all of the firm's clients. Mitchell did not know what to do, so he started a lawsuit to stop Carl from speaking to their clients. Carl did not fight back. He called Mitchell and asked for a meeting. Mitchell refused, given that the matter was in litigation. A judge decided Carl could not be denied his interest in the partnership. By then the law firm had been destroyed.

Even after all the litigation, Carl wanted to have an ordinary conversation with Mitchell. Finally, Mitchell relented. Carl pointed out where an ordinary conversation would have taken them three years earlier. He convinced Mitchell to review the situation through different eyes. He shared what he had seen all along. He put the hard-nosed advocacy into perspective, saying that it was valuable, but only for a narrow class of cases. Mitchell learned. They are partners again.

### Summary

+ Creative resolution is an exercise in group learning.

+ The longer you can stay in a place of "not knowing," the more comprehensive your solution will be.

+ You must keep your mind open to learning facts, concerns, and perspectives of all people involved.

### Reflections

+ Next time you have a situation of conflict, approach it as a learning exercise.

+ See what you can learn about the situation and notice how smart you can get!

# 14

# Becoming
# ResponseAble

| OLD THINKING | NEW THINKING |
|---|---|
| *Deferring to professionals* | *Becoming ResponseAble* |

Some people grow under responsibility, others merely swell.

*Hubbell*

For many of us, some of the operating principles, paradigms, and systems of our culture dilute one of the unique experiences of being human—the privilege of self-consciousness. We have sanitized, professionalized, and diluted some of the interactions that can provide greater self-awareness. Some of us have abdicated personal responsibility for our deepest individual concerns. We do this when we avoid conflict. We stay clear of direct contact with others by delegating to "professionals." We often do this before looking within ourselves for the answers. This has a negative impact because the more we know about who we are the better we can resolve conflict and collaborate with others.

There is a very important distinction here. Going to someone for guidance and education is profound. Looking for help is resourceful. Dropping the situation in someone's lap is not!

## Taking Charge

You may deal with the challenges of conflict by giving it to professionals. You have been taught to believe they know how to do it right! But doing that makes you a spectator in your own life, missing out on the discovery of your own internal and external resolutions, based on your personal standards. In resolving our own conflicts, we can find out who we are, our standards, our boundaries, and the values we are made of. You can remain the captain by becoming **responseAble.** By this I mean that *you* deal with internal and external conflict. You get the direct experience of interacting with other people, human to human, without professionals doing it for you. You get to look at your own conflicts and collaborations. You get to be responsible for the quality of your life experience, instead of having someone dictate that quality based on their standards. On the other side, you don't get someone else to blame. That is little to give up for the gift you receive in return—the gift of yourself and the discovery of knowing more thoroughly what defines you.

The two brothers chose to be responsAble. Rather than abdicating to professionals and allowing a third party to decide for them, they took charge. They chose a form of assistance that helped them get to the core of their conflict. It wasn't pretty, it wasn't nice, it wasn't sanitized—but it was real, and they learned a great deal.

The brothers had the privilege of observing and discovering their feelings, thoughts, reactions, and emotions as they stood toe to toe in a situation that confronted their life. What they learned about themselves would not likely have happened in another forum. Following the old paradigm, they would have been robbed of their life experience. I was proud that they seized the opportunity of learning more about who they were and becoming more emotionally intelligent in the process.[25]

## The Reluctant Father

A couple who had been divorced for five years was involved in a heated child custody and visitation dispute. They had two kids, ages seven and ten. Mom was remarried, and her new husband had a great career opportunity located two states and a four-hour drive away. Mom was intent on moving out of state with their two children. Her former husband was intent on proving that Mom was wrong to leave, although his real concerns were not being mentioned. Dad had never wanted the divorce, so the situation was an opportunity for him to play out his resentment.

The situation was very tense. Under state law, lacking Dad's consent, Mom was required to get the court's permission to move. The opportunity for Mom's new husband would result in a significantly better lifestyle for the kids. They would be living very close to their maternal grandparents and to a school that would provide special programs for the older child, who was gifted. But Dad would not even talk about the benefits of a move.

The court battle reached a watershed when the kids were interviewed in the judge's chambers. Both kids expressed a desire to move. After that, Dad chose responseAbility despite his previous position. He heard the concerns of his children.

The experience of life as a human being is fraught with challenges. It always has been. Given food, shelter, and the absence of predators, our two primary challenges in terms of long-term survival are:

1. Civility—the ability to manage behavior that impacts others

2. Collaboration—the ability to work together.

Becoming responseAble is the key to meeting these challenges.

### Summary

- Deferring to professionals can steal your experience of finding out who you are.

- Your personal identity is revealed as you observe your responses in dealing directly with your own conflicts.

- Dealing directly with your conflicts contributes to your level of emotional intelligence.

### Reflections

- Think of a time that you made a choice to defer to another person or professional.

- What were you feeling at the time? Were you frightened?

- What thoughts and emotions do you have about the outcome?

- Was it resolved to your satisfaction in terms of your emotions? How would you wish the outcome were different?

- Is there an unresolved situation going on in your life right now in which you are not being responsible? What actions could you take that would show greater responsibility on your part? What is the risk of not taking them?

# Part IV

## The Craft of Resolution: A Step-by-Step Guide

*New behaviors are needed if you want improved results. And thinking is definitely a behavior. We made that clear in Part III when we reviewed the ten principles that constitute Resolutionary Thinking. Part IV details the seven steps of the Cycle of Resolution. The goal is to help you develop the craft of moving situations toward resolution. Each chapter discusses one of the steps, using case studies and explaining the dialogues that take you to resolution. Part IV concludes by showing you the connection between the model and the ten principles of new thinking and presenting applications of the new model.*

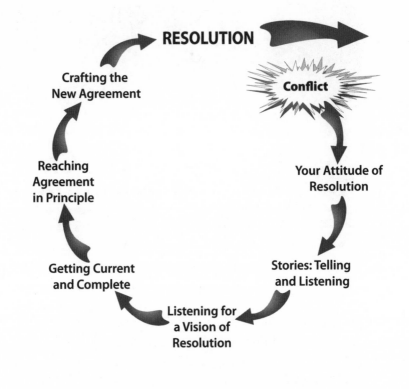

**RESOLUTION**

Conflict

Crafting the
New Agreement

Your Attitude of
Resolution

Reaching
Agreement
in Principle

Getting Current
and Complete

Stories: Telling
and Listening

Listening for
a Vision of
Resolution

# 15

STEP 1
## Your Attitude
## of Resolution

If we keep following the idea of an eye for an eye and a tooth for a tooth, we will end up with an eyeless and toothless world.

*Gandhi*

The first step in the conflict resolution model is developing the attitude of resolution. This means choosing the thinking embodied in the ten principles. The attitude is developed by listening, sharing concerns, and knowing there is an agreement waiting to be discovered. The attitude of resolution is the opposite of thinking about winning or losing.

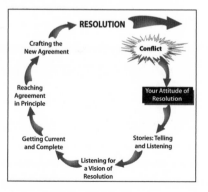

I call the attitude **Resolutionary Thinking.**

Initially, practice, conscious intention, and affirmations will be required to turn the new attitude into a new habit of thinking. To help you develop this new habit, this chapter discusses several skills to use and some obstacles to avoid.

## Adopt an Attitude of Curiosity and Discovery

Embracing an attitude of resolution requires a perspective of curiosity and discovery as you engage in learning more about another person's point of view. Through dialogue you understand what people want and what the situation requires. To stay in the discovering mode, you put aside thinking that you have the "right" answer, "know" what is fair, or have the "truth."

Take a difficult personal situation. Pretend you are not involved. Think about how it is impacting people you care about. From this perspective you can reflect more clearly. Taking on the following behaviors will be very helpful:

1. Respect for everyone and his or her viewpoint

2. Sincerity and open-mindedness in listening

3. Integrity—trustworthiness and fairness

4. Dignity and clarity that you will do well for everyone

5. Authenticity and candor in communication

6. Knowing you have a path to an answer, not the answer

7. Confidence that the resolution will be discovered

8. Centeredness when others lose their cool

9. Humor and tranquility

Stepping into this way of being is not easy or simple, which is why this chapter discusses these behaviors at length. But if you are not sure how to exhibit these behaviors, I suggest you follow the advice that noted therapist Milton Erikson gave to a group of psychiatrists. Erikson told the group to "act as if" they knew what they were doing, until they discovered their own mastery.

## Listen

I recently observed the resolution of an employee claim against a major financial institution. The complaint alleged racial and age discrimination and breaking an employment contract. The situation was resolved in three hours. The key ingredient: listening. Each side told its story in complete detail. The resolutionary listened with impeccable focus. Then he repeated to each person what they had said, almost verbatim. They knew he was listening because of his paraphrasing.

Because everyone was heard in intimate detail, a high level of trust was established. Each side trusted that the resolutionary was their advocate and that their interests would be protected.

There is always common ground. I have come to understand that people, especially intimates, often are on the same side of a conflict. Unfortunately, our use of language in expressing what we feel, and the expectation of opposition, often prevents people from recognizing that there is no disagreement. Listening carefully and asking thoughtful questions can prevent useless conflict. You must listen with more than your ears. You must listen with your eyes and your heart. Always remember that you have one mouth, but two ears.

## Maintain Your Commitment to Resolution

You must believe that resolution is just around the corner—that it will emerge from the next round of communication. The following story illustrates how the commitment to resolution "saved" the lives of a man, a woman, and an unborn child.

*Ron and Elyse.* A colleague, Ron, was in a very difficult love relationship with Elyse. Then they became pregnant. Ron wanted
her to have an abortion. Elyse was clear that she wanted the
child, but because of the acrimony she was not interested in a
long-term relationship with Ron. There were many possibilities
for the couple, but none of the choices seemed satisfactory.

Elyse asked that he pay for the medical costs of the pregnancy and the birth of the child, nothing more. Ron agreed.
But, because Ron was not resolved about the choices they
faced, he wanted to do more, so during the pregnancy Ron
provided things like maternity clothes. As the months passed,
he noticed his inner trouble deepening. Ron was pregnant too,
even though the relationship did not seem viable.

About a month before the child was born, Ron honored
his promises and made his last payment toward the medical
expenses. As soon as he had paid, he was served with a lawsuit
for child support. He felt devastated and betrayed. He called
me to scream, express outrage, and discuss his rights and possible actions. His legal rights were limited, so I suggested writing a letter to Elyse "telling his story." The letter arrived a few
days before the birth. Elyse wasn't interested in what he had to
say. This further inflamed him.

Ron and I strategized. We communicated to Elyse and her
attorney that if they changed the game and had Ron pay child
support, he would be a father to his little girl. He did not do
this out of anger but from his heart. Ron had been considering
taking a larger role, and they had pushed him over the line.
They declined our offer. Ron said that he would still honor the
original agreement (pay medical expenses) or pay child support and be a father, but he would not be exploited.

I met with Elyse's attorney and spoke to her from a place
of clarity and conviction of a vision for the future. Integrity
emerged from my certainty about the best outcome. It seemed

clear (my preliminary vision), given the relationship between Elyse and Ron, that everyone would be better off if the child was brought up by a single parent. The certainty with which I spoke to Elyse's attorney got through. She conferred with Elyse. They agreed to drop their demand for child support if Ron irrevocably surrendered all parental rights to the child.

Even this resolution produced an emotional dilemma for Ron. He had wanted a child, and briefly he had a daughter. I helped guide Ron through his personal agony. Outwardly, I handled the legal questions, negotiations, and agreements. That was a small part of the work.

The real service was the attitude of resolution I brought to the situation by guiding Ron through conflict to a resolution of what he would do, given his choices and his emotions about those choices. The choices had far less to do with anything outside himself—lawyers, lawsuits, money—than with his own values, beliefs, and emotions. Aside from the resolution, something very important happened for Ron. He had never felt so supported. He learned about the value of a guide who was committed to his well-being.

When you are facing a difficult situation, do not waver in your belief that it will be resolved.

## Sit Down and Talk

The way to resolve conflict and build relationships is through effective communication: plain talk about real concerns, not piecemeal sharing of information packaged for winning or to satisfy the requirements of a legal proceeding. When lawyers tell their clients to stop talking to the other side, they ensure there will be no resolution until the legal proceedings are over.

A corporate counsel for a Fortune 100 company has made starting a lawsuit an arduous task for his lawyers. The lawyers must first document that they have taken almost heroic measures to resolve the matter in the least invasive way. This process was put in place because it was often easier for a lawyer to file suit than to show the "weakness and vulnerability" of just talking to the other side. In this case, the internal documentation required to justify filing suit is more onerous than opening a dialogue with "the enemy." This company's practice contributes to resolution. The motivation is economy and efficiency. It works, and it conserves resources.

### Have Fun!

It is important to have fun with an attitude of resolution. I do! Laugh at yourself as you disarm people committed to a fight. Watch their faces drop and their bodies relax when you listen and speak from a mood of resolution. Gandhi was right when he said that the British couldn't win if 80 million Indians wouldn't fight. Ghandi's stance demonstrated that, although it seems counter-intuitive, it takes two people to have a fight, but just one to end it. This works, even with the thorniest adversary. Prove to yourself that most people don't want to fight; it's a learned response.

A mood of civility leads to relationships that resolve things. When you declare that you want resolution, the mood of the dialogue shifts from a battle to collaboration. Even if you're pretending at first, it will become effective. It will become real very quickly when you see the results.

I counsel clients to go directly to the source of the breakdown: the person they are fighting with. First I evaluate their attitude and do my best to engender a mood of resolution. I try to change their expectation about the outcome.

For example, Manuel was being threatened by his former company. They were headed to court to prevent his soliciting any of their clients. But Manuel was an independent contractor, and he had no employment contract restricting what he did. Meanwhile his old company owed him more than $20,000 in commissions.

Coaching him to hold a mood of resolution helped. Manuel received every dollar without litigation or further threat of any kind because he was able to approach the matter with a mood of resolution. You can have the same result. Think in terms of getting to resolution, not winning. Don't think about your position; think of a fair resolution for everyone.

## Obstacles to Achieving an Attitude of Resolution

Working against your achieving an attitude of resolution are aspects of old paradigm thinking—legal standards, legal rights, and what is considered "truth."

### Legal Standards

What participants in a conflict think is "fair" is a far more useful standard for resolution than what the law might dictate.

Recently the CEO of a multibillion dollar public utility paid $25 million in damages to an eight-year-old boy who was almost electrocuted. Despite his lawyer's advice that he was not legally responsible, the CEO felt that the right thing to do was make a quick payment. He was following a different standard. The following fable illustrates the point.

A Middle Eastern couple was having severe marital problems. Fatima wanted a divorce; Ali was torn by the conflict between his wife and his mother. It was customary in the culture for a man to provide living quarters for his mother after his father died. Not only did the mother live with her son, she also got to pick her quarters. Ali's mother occupied the main floor apartment of a two-story house. The second story was occupied by Fatima and Ali. In order for Fatima to get to her quarters, she had to pass through her mother-in-law's apartment. Every time she did, she was berated for one reason or another. Her patience was exhausted.

Ali did not want to be disrespectful to his mother, and he did not want to lose his wife. He did not know what to do. Fatima and Ali went before the town elder and each told their story.

Fatima spoke of her frustration and anger; Ali spoke of being pulled in opposite directions by the two women he loved. After hearing both sides, the elder, with a twinkle in his eye, proposed a resolution. He suggested that they obtain a ladder so Fatima could enter her apartment without confronting her mother-in-law. It worked. That's resolution! No thought was wasted about who was right and who was wrong or what the legal standard was. The elder just designed a practical, effective solution.

A famous mediator shared his experience of returning to the family law firm after getting all As in his first year of Harvard Law School. He was bragging to his uncle about his performance in contracts and criminal law when his 88-year-old grandfather asked him how he did in "settlements." As mentioned in the preface, the most effective attorneys know that resolution, not winning, is what's important.

### Rights

Your rights are usually not the most important aspect of a situation. Emotion, past relationships, and future collaborations must be considered. Especially important is the kind of relationship you want in the future. Thinking only about today may not serve you.

If you know a situation will change, take that into account. In a recent divorce, I sensed my client would be in another relationship before too long. I suggested she accept a "discounted" one-time payment instead of periodic alimony payments that would be cut off if she remarried or lived with someone. This tack prevented a brewing battle about whether she would receive alimony for the rest of her life. Even though she had rights, it was smarter not to push them.

### Truth

You probably think that the truth is very important. There are, however, many truths in every situation! Truth is usually elusive, sometimes irrelevant, and always dependent upon who's evaluating and their standard. I believe that people want the "more than truth" that resolution provides, because often everyone has a different truth.

When I started practicing law, I believed there was *a* truth that you could find in the courtroom. I was representing a client who was injured in a motorcycle accident. He had one story about what had happened. The driver of the other vehicle had a different story. The eyewitnesses had another story, as did the investigating officer. After listening to the stories I was convinced each one was telling the truth. Everyone had a different picture. No one was lying. As I learned more perception, I learned *a* truth about truth: everyone has his or her truth, and often there is no one truth.

A magistrate was presented with a case of a contract to sell a house. He listened to the eloquent owner and said "You're right." He listened to the equally impressive buyer and said "You're right." When both sides confronted him with his inconsistency he said "You're right." The truth doesn't always set you free!

## When They Won't Cooperate

A question I am frequently asked in my workshops is how to achieve an attitude of resolution where people have dug in their heels, or have difficult personalities, or have more power in the situation than you have. This is a subject many people find challenging and frustrating. There are no easy answers, and sometimes people won't budge, but here are the suggestions that have worked for me:

1. Honor their position and their personality—make friends with them. Fighting and resisting will get you nowhere. When you push against a force, it will push back against you with greater intensity. Better to be empathetic and gain an understanding of where they are coming from and how they got to that place. Once you understand them, you can form a strategy to get them to the table.

2. Show them the cost of the current situation and the ongoing cost of no resolution. Use the cost of conflict analysis in Chapter 2 to demonstrate the ongoing enormous loss they are suffering.

3. Show them the potential benefit of the creative solution you have in mind. Let them see what they stand to gain and demonstrate your awareness of their concerns.

4. Have the resolution show up as their idea. People sometimes resist an idea that is not theirs. If you lead them to where the idea becomes theirs, they buy in more easily. You can do this by asking questions.

5. Appeal to a higher authority. Is there someone with more influence than you to whom the resistant party will listen

and honor, such as a boss, public official, legal provision, moral authority, or the like? You don't get a prize for doing it by yourself.

6. Ask yourself about whether you are seeing the situation from their perspective. In other words, are you out of line, and is their "unreasonableness" justified?

Don't give up, no matter what. The only way you get to resolution is by taking the journey. Remember, sometimes the hardest part is getting them to the table. That said, there are times when cutting your losses is the best strategy. *Where is the edge?* you might ask. Experience will tell you, and if you are smart and have enough experience you'll know.

### Summary

• The attitude you carry about conflict is a threshold that determines how easy it will be for you to accomplish what you desire.

• Listening and "learning" your way to the discovery and design of effective resolutions are essential skills.

• Paying too much attention to rights, legal standards, and "the truth" will often promote conflict.

• Adopting the attitude of "knowing" that a fair resolution can be found is a keystone for finding it.

• Discovering resolution can be as simple as an ordinary conversation, if you can let go of the need to be right and be willing to accept what is most effective for the future.

### Reflections

• Choose two situations of conflict in your life. Decide to take action in each of them.

- In one, try to prove that you are right; go for winning. In the other, take on the attitude of resolution and inquiry.

- How do they differ in outcome? In emotion? In terms of long-term relationships?

# 16

## Stories: Telling and Listening

When we haven't the time to listen to each other's stories we seek out experts to teach us how to live. The less time we spend together at the kitchen table, the more how-to books appear in the stores and on our bookshelves. . . . Because we have stopped listening to each other we may even have forgotten how to listen, stopped learning how to recognize meaning. . . .

*Rachel Naomi Remen, MD*[26]

We all want to tell "our" story. Reciting it, uninterrupted, to an engaged listener serves an essential, cathartic purpose. It is an important information-gathering vehicle for all concerned. This includes the storyteller, who learns

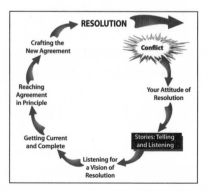

from listening to his or her own story. That is why the first action step in the Cycle of Resolution is the opportunity for each participant to tell their story from beginning to end, without interruption. This gives everyone the time to get their unique perspective out on the table. Conflict is created in the mind of each person involved as a story they tell themselves about the situation. As long as their story goes untold it remains trapped inside.

Allowing the story to emerge is a critical part of the process. When we interrupt those who have a story to tell by asking questions we think are critical we are effectively cutting off their catharsis and depriving ourselves of deeply knowing what they are thinking. We must also remember to listen to the stories they tell. I have learned over time that when we tell our stories publicly they come out differently from the stories we tell ourselves—and the public stories are closer to what really happened.

The way I usually begin the interactive process is to tell people that we all hold conflict inside in the form of a the story we tell ourselves about the situation. Then I ask everyone to tell their story. Getting everyone's story out on the table defines the problem space, validates everyone's position, and reveals everyone's interests.

## More Important Than Winning

My favorite illustration of the importance of telling the story comes from a lawyer in Canada. He had just finished a hearing before a judge. Although his client was with him, the matter was decided on legal theory and sworn affidavits; there was no need for his client to testify.

After two hours of reviewing exhibits, hearing legal arguments, and engaging in hotly contested advocacy, my Canadian friend prevailed and won a $500,000 judgment for his client. He was very pleased and considered this a great victory. After the judge excused himself, my friend turned to his client and, with an unusual display of effusiveness said, "Isn't that great? We just won half a million," to which his client replied with great disappointment, "But I never got to tell my story." The need to tell his story was as important as the financial victory.

We need to tell our stories. We need to have others hear our stories. Winning is not the only thing; *and* it is not everything.

When you initially become involved in resolving a conflict, it is essential to listen to the story, the whole story, in the way the other person wants to tell it. Listen as if you were listening to a lover you do not want to lose who is threatening to leave. Make the other person feel that he or she has never been listened to before in the way you are listening now. Whether you are a participant or facilitator, remember that when someone tells their story, a change occurs for both the listener and the storyteller.

## Professional Service

One arena in which it is essential to air stories fully is the establishment of a professional service relationship. Often the service providers do not get to the other person's real concerns because they listen to themselves and their notion of what's wrong or what needs to be done; or they listen through their professional filter and miss the full story. This is true whether it's a relationship with a therapist, physician, lawyer, accountant, consultant, contractor, auto mechanic, or home-repair person.

When you listen to the full story at the beginning, you avoid a host of future difficulties, and you enable yourself to get much closer to providing exceptional customer service. Taking the time to let people fully air what is on their mind is a key ingredient in resolving their concerns and reaching their desired outcome.

## Software Designers Who Told Their Story

*George and Luke.* George and Luke were software designers who had been working on the same project for seven years. George was a creative genius with broad-ranging design ability. Luke was an engineer by training and experience whose primary talent was his ability to keep moving forward. Each had a team of product developers whom they tried to inspire. George and Luke wanted to be role models for the people who worked for them.

Most of the time, when George and Luke worked together, things went smoothly. But during the last two years, George had decided that Luke's "plodding" style was hindering their creativity. He "knew" genius was demonstrated by intuitive flashes of brilliance and the epiphany of creative insight. At the same time, Luke became more firmly convinced that great leaps forward, although they sometimes had aspects of the intuitive, were essentially derived from rigorously and consistently applying principles and practices.

These stylistic variants went largely unnoticed until George and Luke were summoned by Maya, the CEO. She had just finished negotiating a make-or-break-the-company deal. Maya was not sure she could deliver on her promises. The desired results required a team effort. George and Luke would have to work in tandem. But they had no respect for each other! For two years they had spent each day in a private war. Now, their jobs and their company's survival were at stake.

Luke asked Jack, a senior human resources consultant, to

help get them to the other side of their war. Although he held little hope of friendship and true collaboration, Luke saw a chance of developing a working relationship. Jack said he was up to the task, but he wanted to ruminate on the question of how to do it for a few days. Jack decided the only way to start down the path to resolution was to bring George and Luke together and have each tell his story. Since both of them respected Jack, a safe environment had been set up. In this situation there was nothing to lose.

As George and Luke recited their stories, each gained information, new respect, and appreciation for the other. Both were surprised to hear what the other thought about their approach to the work process. Each listened attentively as the other told his "truths," perceptions, observations, and predictions for the future.

Jack told George and Luke they would both be served if they suspended their judgments as much as they could. This was not a request to stop making judgments; that's part of our fabric and we all do it naturally. Rather, it was a request to "observe" the judgments and not immediately accept them as the truth. This is important, though it's not easy. Rather than defend yourself or make the other person wrong, listen so you can understand the other's reality.

When George and Luke returned to work, they had gained a new understanding of the other's capacity and competence. The genius of each person came through in his story. In sharing who they were, what they observed, and what they did, they put in place conditions for the best use of their talents. When it came time to make assignments for the project, George and Luke wasted no time in assigning themselves what they did best and requesting the other's help in areas where he was brilliant. The more they worked together, the more respect they gained for each other.

The stories of Luke and George allowed each person to be heard and legitimized. How many times have you had an initial impression that shifted when you had a greater experience of someone? Please remember that.

## The Manager Who Could Listen

In the early 1980s, shortly after the break-up of the Bell system, Jose found out that one of his salesmen, Shelly, was on a task force involved with a new telecommunications application. Jose was furious. He was never asked for his approval, and he did not think the application made economic sense. He called Shelly into his office and told him not to have anything more to do with the task force.

Shelly was a self-confident independent thinker. He was not sure why Jose had taken the position he had, or what to do about it. Shelly did not like being told what to do, but instead of telling Jose where to go, he decided to sleep on it. Shelly had chosen the project because he felt strongly about its economies of scale. He believed in the project and wanted to be a part of its implementation.

Early the next morning Shelly went to Jose's office and told his own story, about why he wanted to be involved. He told how the project made sense and why it was the wave of the future. The group Shelly wanted to join was pushing into new territory. The members would be "intrapreneurs," designing their own marketing, sales, and implementation material. They would be scavenging for needed resources. They would be out from under the bureaucracy.

Shelly convinced Jose that the potential rewards were worth the risks. His open self-disclosure reached Jose's heart as he told a story from his own heart. Shelly revealed himself, and Jose responded favorably. Shelly's zeal was not misplaced.

The project served as a model for corporate "intrapreneurial" action, and Shelly and his team were asked to train hundreds of managers in how they achieved their goals. Shelly learned the value of telling your story; Jose learned to listen!

## Telling the Story of a Marriage

In marriage, the opportunity to tell the story is the opportunity to heal the breach. Coming clean, telling your truth, is the first step in the resolution. That's where healing begins. From your truth comes the authenticity that leads to new resolution.

A few years ago I was called into a situation everyone thought was hopeless. Jim and Irene had been married for five hard years. Each felt honor-bound to go the distance, no matter how difficult their day-to-day lives and no matter how the long-term prospects dulled the potential for an actualized life. Though their relationship did not work, they were more concerned with doing what they thought was the right thing than what would make them happy. Compared to what was possible, they were prisoners of their beliefs.

I was asked to see them under the guise of an ongoing disagreement about vacations. Irene wanted to go camping, and Jim wanted to stay at the Plaza in New York. I had brief conversations with each of them, and upon meeting them my intuition was confirmed. This couple did not want to be together. I say this knowing we can never understand what draws two people together—but this relationship looked like a mismatch.

My real service was to get them to talk about what was going on beneath the surface. I provided a buffer and an opening. The conversation took off. Each told a story of compromise, deprivation, and longing for a different, more authentic life. Because they were given a forum to tell their story, two lives were salvaged.

## Kid Stuff

Rachel was having a difficult time with her eight-year-old. Ralph had been a model child. One day when Rachel picked him up at school he got in the car, slammed the door, and said, "I hate that place!" Rachel started criticizing his conduct. This dialogue was repeated for five straight days. Rachel had even screamed at Ralph and demanded that he change his behavior. He would not listen. Ralph was angry!

After consulting with her therapist friend, Rachel tried a new tactic. In a calm and reassuring voice she asked Ralph what was wrong and why he hated the place. Because of the opening Rachel provided, Ralph felt safe enough to speak. He told his story. Every day he was being teased by the boys in his class about the way he was dressed. The comments were creating a conflict. Because the comments were directed at trousers selected by Rachel, he feared that if he told Rachel she would feel bad. It was easier to hate the place than deal with his inner conflict.

Rachel was thrilled that Ralph told her his story. It was easy to purchase different trousers. Listening to the story changed the outcome. Ralph no longer hates school. He no longer complains. He has stopped slamming doors. Telling and listening to stories goes a long way toward resolving difficulties you experience with kids. Children are people living within their own stories that must be honored and respected.

How often have you told yourself a story because it was easier than dealing with a difficult conflict? As we move to the interactive model of the book, two important contexts need mention. The first is timeless, the second required by our time.

## Communication Skills

Many books already exist detailing what to do and what not to do to be an effective communicator. Your communication skills will impact the value and outcome of the resolution process. It is easy to imagine certain behaviors alienating a participant, no matter how good the process is. If you suspect you have communications problems, do consult books specifically on the subject. For now, here are a few hints:

*Moving through roadblocks.* Good communicators do not give up until their message is delivered.

*No difficult people, only different people.* Many instruments demonstrate differences clearly.

*Developing emotional intelligence.* This is a critical collaborative skill.

*Responding and reacting.* Choose what you say based on a longer-term vision for the future.

*Anger and aggression.* Neither is effective.

*"I" statements.* Speak from your feeling in response to their behavior.

*Know/do/feel.* Be clear of the outcome you want from what you say.

*Mirroring/identifying.* Creating rapport goes a long way.

*Don't bark back at barking dogs.* Talking louder only leads to louder talking.

*Listening skills.* These are the critical skills.

*Object/subject.* Treat others as people.

*Non-verbal messages.* Be aware that when we are face to face, 90% of our messages are non-verbal.

## Working Virtually

The way people interact and communicate has changed. The frequency and availability of face-to-face (**f2f**) communication has been dramatically curtailed. This physical reality requires a greater level of consciousness about our communication because so many of our messages are no longer delivered personally. Taking away the visual, tone, and energy of interactions demands a new communications consciousness.

When we deliver messages in the f2f world, what we convey is transmitted in the following proportions: 55% visual appearance, 38% tone or mood, and 7% word content. More than 90% of what we "say" is communicated non-verbally.[27] Given that virtual-world communication is often text-based, it becomes critical to add description and feeling tone to our messages. We need substitutes for the usual layers of visual and auditory cues typical of our personal chats. Equally important is the need to quickly switch communication channels depending on the kind of conversation you are having. It becomes critical to "listen" very carefully to what is written.

Text message, e-mail, voice mail, cell phone, and video conference—all are available. Think about the nature of the interaction, its importance, the participants, and your objectives, and then make a deliberate choice about the channel you use. The more personal and intimate, the more "bandwidth," unless things are so hot between people that a buffer is useful.

On the surface the various cultural subgroups have unique characteristics: race, religion, national origin, gender, age, values, work habits, communication patterns, to name a few. Although these characteristics appear to create differences among people, they are not the entire story. Remember that beneath the surface we are more similar than different. We need to become culturally multi-lingual in the way we communicate.

### Summary

- The second step in resolving conflict is to listen carefully to all of the stories in the situation, including your own.

- Remember, listening benefits the other people involved as well as you, so let them have the experience of telling their story without interruption.

- Just because you don't respond does not mean you agree. At this stage your task is gathering information, and finding out the other person's reality about the situation.

- Effective communication skills, f2f and virtual, contribute to resolution.

### Reflections

- Most of us don't listen. We are waiting impatiently to speak or thinking about what we're going to say.

- To give yourself some insight into the value of listening, spend a day in silence, just listening to the stories in your surroundings. Put a sign around your neck saying, "I'm not speaking today, just listening!"

# 17

# Listening
## for a Vision
## of Resolution

Only he who can see the invisible can do the impossible.

*Frank L. Gaines*

Engaging in a process of resolution ignites sparks of creativity, and telling stories puts that creativity into play. The attitude of resolution illuminates a path on which resolution is discovered.

The content of each side's story is the crucible that holds the potential for a solution honoring the concerns of all parties.

The potential resolution emerges in the same way that a "third body" is revealed when two individuals are in an intimate

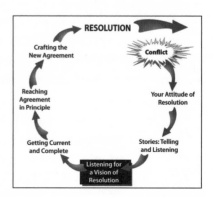

relationship. This third body has a viability of its own, born from the shared energy of all those involved. No individual can do this alone because each person has only an individual input. It's why talking to yourself about a difficult situation often leads nowhere; you keep spinning through the same thought process. Exposing the story to air creates a very different result. The conflict needs to be viewed through a different lens. The alchemical fusion that takes place when stories are shared is both predictable and unpredictable. You know it will lead to a resolution, but you don't know what the solution will be.

Whether you are a neutral third party (professional facilitator, friend, or manager) or one of the participants, as you listen to all the stories, you begin to sense the best solution. This requires detachment from thoughts of winning or proving you are right. The visions of the future are the source of the new reality that is emerging. This vision attracts the energy and resources that will make it happen. This preliminary vision is the third step in the Model of Resolution. In situations that don't carry a great deal of emotional baggage, it's possible to move to resolution after people tell their stories. It is nice when it happens, but you cannot count on it or drive to it. In fact, a common mistake is to jump to solution before people are ready. When a situation is filled with emotion you must get to the bottom of that heat, the real source of the conflict, otherwise the solution will blow up.

In traditional wisdom among conflict resolution professionals, remaining neutral means not having a vision of the outcome; that vision is up to the people involved. However, try as you may, you *will* have a vision! Your mind just does that. An effective resolutionary does have a vision of the outcome, whether participant or resolutionary. You must be careful, especially as a beginner, not to become too attached, or drive the result to your vision. As new facts, perceptions, concerns, and motivations are revealed, your vision of the resolution may change. Remember, your vision is not as important as their vision. But neutrality means being fair and impartial, not lacking involvement. I suggest you keep your vision of the outcome in check in case the participants reach an impasse. Then you might gently offer a suggestion.

## Follow Your Instincts

The preliminary vision of resolution has its seed in feelings of fairness. The vision is intuitive, beyond the logic that will come later to justify it. It is the kernel around which a full resolution is formed, just as a pearl grows from the irritation of a grain of sand. Our logical minds will find the rational basis to validate what our intuition and emotion already know.

In this step of the model, faith and trust are very important. **Trust** is about listening to your deepest instincts. First, you listen to all the stories. Then, from a sense of fairness, and taking care of everyone's concerns, you will likely have some undefined sense of where the situation might go. You get an idea of whether two business partners should stay together, whether a commercial relationship is viable, or what the best use of a city's resources would be. It is important to listen to that intuitive voice. It's not necessarily right, but it will provide a starting perspective that others can react to.

**Faith** is the faith to keep following your intuition even though you are not sure exactly why. The best-selling author Scott Peck said that when he was younger he was often unclear about why he would do certain things or follow a certain path. He learned to have faith and follow his instincts in the process. Eventually the logic and reasons were revealed.[28]

In the "two brothers" story in Chapter 3, I had a vision of brotherly cooperation. I held that vision gently as an operational thesis as the process of resolution unfolded. Either brother could have held that position. Holding the vision as a beacon helped enable the result. I did not know the particular details, but I had a clear sense that resolution must include the perspective of brotherly cooperation. People in the midst of conflict usually are holding onto some past emotion. It may be up to a third person, or one of the participants who is ready to move into the future, to hold the new perspective. It's understandable for people to hold onto the past. The next stop of the model is designed to help people move through their resistance.

*Rick.* Rick was a manic-depressive who had lost his fortune in the stock market mini-crash of 1987. He was ready to jump off a bridge. I sensed it was more important to deal with Rick's tenuous emotional state than with a lawsuit he might bring against his broker. I started painting a vision for the future: even if he recovered nothing in his lawsuit, he would be OK. I also had to deal with his vision of holding himself at fault—his seeing the situation as just more evidence of his own incompetence. I held a vision of his accepting the loss, doing what he could to recover financially, and forgiving himself for whatever he thought he did wrong. That came from trusting my intuition about a vision I had for the future.

## Testing Your Intuition

Intuitions and feelings that reflect a sense of fairness about the resolution are the starting point of your preliminary vision, a starting point from which you can test whether, and how, other pieces fit together. Trusting this enabled me to resolve the 25 Camden Legal Services cases I mentioned at the beginning of the book. To test your preliminary vision and generate discussion about it among the participants, you can ask the following questions.

1. *Does the preliminary vision fit everyone's view of the outcome?* Find out early everyone's vision for the outcome.

2. *Does the preliminary vision take care of all specific concerns in the situation?* Everyone has important and unique concerns and interests that must be accommodated in the resolution.

3. *What needs correcting or adjusting?* In what ways is your vision off? How will the resolution need to shift to accommodate considerations you did not address? If anyone's vision is far from your preliminary vision, you may have to shift your expectation. You will have to understand other visions and begin the educational process that will enable everyone to understand the wisdom and benefits of different perspectives.

4. *What do others say about your preliminary vision's viability?* If you listen to others, you will find out all you need to know about whether your vision is workable. What they say will point to needed changes or to things they do not understand that must be explained.

5. *What concerns or fears does your preliminary vision bring up?* This is another way to find out what is missing from your vision. Because concerns or fears often stem from incomplete information, what further information must you provide to have others say yes to your projected outcome? Salespeople will understand this as "handling objections."

6. *What or who is missing?* The situation may call for pivotal additional information or the presence of a missing

party. It is important to make sure that what is missing is brought into the situation.

7. *What must be learned or discovered to test your vision?* Is there some test that must be performed or a premise that must be validated? What needs to be set in motion to accomplish that? Perhaps the conflict is based on incorrect information.

8. *Is it a comfortable place from which to move forward?* Having shared your vision and listened to all that has been said to this point, are you and all parties comfortable in moving forward? Are you ready to take the next steps knowing what you know? Are you confident you can reach resolution?

9. *Who else has suggestions or insights about anything anyone has said?* Even though you have a vision you think is brilliant, it is essential to listen and keep listening to the views and thoughts of others. As you hear what they say, you might learn something valuable because of the way they present information or because of your readiness to hear it. The important point is to stay in the inquiry for as long as you can.

Resolutions that I have helped facilitate as a lawyer, mediator, and consultant often came from a clear vision I had of the outcome. I arrived at that vision after I listened to and understood everyone's concerns. I have come to know that interests and concerns are like feelings; they are not right or wrong, they just *are*. It was not an outcome that I wanted for myself; it was the outcome I thought was fair for everyone. That premise always guided my actions, and I was always open to learning why it wasn't viable. Determining viability is the purpose of asking the preceding questions.

## Customer Focus

Sharon called Caleb with serious concerns about the computer system he had installed the week before. The system was designed to bring a 600-bed hospital into the twenty-first century. Caleb was the principal salesperson and, as team leader, was also responsible for the installation. Caleb's team included representatives from other departments of the manufacturer. Sharon was the hospital administrator. Right now the system was frustrating the hospital staff.

Caleb's worst fears were realized. For the past month, members of his team had been bickering. Each department knew that *its* way to install and repair the system was the *right* way. Units were not concerned with the system working, only with their own narrow sphere and with not being blamed for the problems. Even though Caleb held meetings to remind everyone that the hospital and patients' lives were the primary concern, Caleb's team members would not put aside their individual concerns to build consensus about the optimal way to proceed.

Although his job was at stake, Caleb felt compelled to call his division VP, Scott Branch. Scott called all the unit heads who would be needed to fix the problems. Lives were at stake. The situation had to be fixed. Quickly! Within an hour the team was assembled. Caleb briefed Scott as they waited for everyone to arrive. Scott started the meeting by saying that his concern was the customer, their patients, and the business of saving lives and making people well. He held a vision of the system working efficiently. He acted as facilitator and motivator, never using his authority.

Scott spent some time clearing the air. He asked all participants to approach anyone with whom they were angry. The conversations that followed were not pleasant, but they were effective in getting everyone beyond their selfish frames of reference and lack of concern for other team members and other departments.

Holding his vision of resolution, Scott attacked the multi-faceted problem. He set up a procedure for evaluating each problem and choosing a plan of action. As each problem was presented, every team captain spoke to the problem and the best way to resolve it. They built consensus as to the best course of action. By now everyone was beyond individual petty concerns and focused on the customer. Everyone's "game" had shifted from being right to the creativity of discovering resolution.

By 1 PM a course of action was charted and by 2 PM, crews were in place implementing the plan. By 4 PM, miracles started to happen. By 6 PM, the system was under control, and by 8 PM everything was functioning within tolerable limits of the promised specifications. The source of the resolution was the clear vision Scott held of everything working well.

## Aligning Vision and Expectations

My sister had just gone through a very difficult divorce after more than 20 years of marriage. As things started to get ugly, I wanted to help. I held the vision of a reasonable resolution. Being intimately involved and having seen the messy course a divorce can take, I was sure the situation could be resolved simply. I was wrong!

There was too much emotional baggage for the reasonable resolution I envisioned. Actually, that is not completely accurate: The ultimate resolution matched my vision, but their way of getting to resolution was much different from mine. They ended up going through a dozen court hearings, countless trips to the courthouse, and scores of telephone calls with lawyers.

It reminded me of what I had realized early in my career as a practicing attorney. In most situations you have a given set of facts and a defined context, which includes the controlling legal and environmental constraints. These are givens that do not change. To the facts and the context must be added a set of individual, personal expectations. A professional has little impact on the context or the facts; they represent a predictable range of results. The area that *can* be influenced is people's expectations. I always try to influence expectations because I know the difference between the expectation and the predictable range of outcome holds the greatest potential for producing unhappiness.

As a mediator and consultant, I have always honored that reality. Getting the vision in line with expectations will always produce satisfaction.

### *Summary*

- A preliminary vision about the resolution will usually come up after everyone has a chance to tell their own story.

- Trust your intuition that the vision that comes up is a good place to start a dialogue.

- If you are part of the conflict, make sure your vision contains everyone's concerns.

- Be careful not to jump to the solution too quickly.

### *Reflections*

- Think of a situation that is bothering you.

- If you take into account the concerns of everyone in the situation by walking in everyone's shoes, what is your vision of a fair outcome?

- Propose your solution and let everyone know how it meets their concerns. What is their reaction?

# 18

STEP 4
# Getting Current
and Complete

He that cannot forgive others, breaks the bridge over which
he must pass himself; for every man has need to be forgiven.

*Lord Herbert*

Getting current and complete is a pivotal step in the model of
resolution. But before discussing the "how to" of the completion process, it is impor-
tant to understand how it
serves the process of resolution.[29]

## Purposes of the
Completion Process

Much is revealed by you
and to you during the

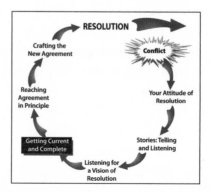

completion process, and a great deal happens internally that helps build consensus. Often you hold onto a preliminary vision because you believe a particular position is right. After the completion process, you may view the situation differently. When you understand that the others in the situation are not the enemy, that they likely want the same general outcome as you, and that their perspective and position is legitimate even though you may not agree with it, resolution becomes possible.

The completion process serves a number of very important purposes.

### *Disclosure*

The primary purpose of disclosure is to ensure that everyone has disclosed all the information they have about the situation. The process extracts a complete picture, with all of the internal dialogue and attached emotional impact. In contrast to sharing a story in response to an open-ended question, the completion process involves asking specific questions designed to elicit feelings and emotions about the story that emerge popcorn style.

In both business and personal situations, it is essential for all involved to participate authentically if they want to get to resolution. I make that request at the beginning. If people are not committed to being authentic, why waste everyone's time? People are often concerned, especially in business, that there may be adverse consequences from complete disclosure. But in a lawsuit, you are compelled to disclose everything as information is "discovered" by the other side. Completion works best when everyone understands that the benefits are worth the risk of openness and disclosure. Otherwise, you waste productivity because of hidden, private motives.

### Getting Current

The second purpose is revealed in the name of the step: completion. The past is brought to the present so you can move into the future. You have said all that can be said about the matter up to that moment in time. All internal chatter is out in the open. You declare that the matter is "complete" and is now behind you. Now you face forward and design the specifics of the new agreement that will govern the relationship in the future.

### *The Alchemy of Emotion*

Third, and most important, the questions of the completion process ensure that you go deeper into your feelings and emotions about the situation. The process provides a safe context for you to articulate things that are highly charged. During the completion process, the alchemy of resolution takes place. The other's concerns and vulnerability are fully revealed. You cross over a point on your internal continuum between the desire to be right and your sense of compassion about the situation. What surfaces is the natural human desire to take care of the concerns of a business partner, friend, colleague, or family member, even if you are presently in conflict. The shared emotion of vulnerability makes possible a new agreement and a new form of collaboration that can give you the benefit of your original expectation, when everyone can see that is still possible. It happens—between colleagues, business partners, and spouses. This process enables the internal work that is pivotal for reaching the next step in the process—an agreement in principle.

### *Letting Go*

In the alchemy of emotions discussed above, the crossover to feeling compassion in the conflict is fostered by the attitude of resolution. When the third-party facilitator, or the participant leading the completion process, internalizes the attitude of resolution by rising above personal concerns about winning and being right, everyone benefits. It's why the attitude of resolution embodied in the ten principles is so important.

In addition to being a participant, you may become a warrior—a champion for resolution. You have the wisdom and experience to see the resolution taking form, and you gently guide yourself and others to that place. If you stay open-minded, you can lead others to a resolution, even though it might not be exactly where you thought. Everyone is learning about the current status of the situation and all their deepest feelings about it. The more authentic, open-hearted, and honest you can be as you reflect about what is said, the more satisfying the outcome. Completion enables you to walk in the other's shoes. That is the key to getting to resolution. It frames, provides the container, and is the aim of the completion process. Getting people to see how holding on costs them is often an inducement that creates the awareness and realization of how much control each individual has. Forgiveness is much more about you than them; it's a gift you give yourself, not them. In forgiving you are moving beyond the conflict.

## The Completion Process

What follows is a description of the process and the conversational steps that must take place. At each step, all parties speak until they have no more to say. It works best when done at a brisk pace, just saying what comes to mind, without filtering or trying to be nice. There is no discussion, just speaking and listening. Candor is essential. The intention is to experience a cleansing expression, a letting go.

Although I discuss the specific steps as though they were being administered by a third-party facilitator, the process can be facilitated by a participant. The process also can be self-administered for use with internal conflict. For that I suggest you speak aloud so you can listen to what you are saying, or write it in a journal.

The steps in the completion process can be taken using two options. Option One is best suited for more intimate relationships (long-term partners, close colleagues, married couples, or family members) or when there is the desire or necessity of a continuing long-term relationship. Option Two is for more formal business environments. The statement and specific questions to be answered for each option are listed below, followed by explanatory material. The explanatory material can be told to the participants verbatim, or it can be paraphrased. After each question is answered, a "file" should be created in your mind that contains the conversation. That file can be "stored" or "deleted."

### *Option One—For Intimate or Ongoing Relationships*

If you are ready to envision a new agreement for your future relationship, it is important to bring your relationship into the present.

It is essential for you to commit to the future and to participate fully in this process. The deeper, more vulnerable, OPEN, and authentic your disclosures, the easier it will be to get to resolution. Listening carefully, to yourself and to others, is important. Understand that others live in a different reality than you. What they say may not be *the* truth, but it is *their* truth. Please don't respond or discuss what is being said. Just speak or listen. You will get your chance to respond if you must.

## 1. What worked about the relationship, partnership, or venture?

You must say everything that worked about the relationship. This will force you to reflect and remember better times—the aspects of the relationship that were productive and satisfying. Your holding the other person as an enemy dissipates when you focus on what worked. You realize the value of the relationship that you once shared, and the value of the "other."

## 2. What didn't work?

It is important to hear what the other person says did not work. In a reflective and quiet mood, start to become accountable for your participation in the breakdown. You will begin to see how you might have done it differently, how your actions might have violated the other person's standards and concerns, and what new actions you might take. This is useful for the future of the relationship and for your own growth and learning. As a facilitator what you hear will inform what a new agreement needs to address.

Somewhere in the next two steps, internal resolution will take place! Anger and righteousness cannot occupy the same space as forgiveness and gratitude! You will have to work very hard to resist resolution.

## 3. Who do you need to forgive and for what?

The purpose of this section is to get you to let go of the anger you are holding. Forgiving others, and yourself, enables you to let go of what you have tied up in the past. You are then free to move into the future. Just saying the words doesn't make it so, but the intention and declaration is an excellent beginning.

### 4.   Who do you need to apologize to, and for what?

Apology is one of the most powerful actions one can take in moving through a conflict.

### 5.   Who do you need to thank, and for what?

This part of the process enables you to go through the breakdown and get into honoring and legitimizing others. It forces you to see the value others have brought. It's hard to hold onto your anger and blame when you step into a mood of gratitude for what they did. All should both forgive and thank themselves!

### 6.   What else do you need to say so that you are complete enough to say "Today is a good day to die"?

This is a catchall that provides the opportunity to say anything that has not been said. It is part of the Lakota warrior blessing ritual. Before a war party set out, the holy man would ask each warrior if it was a good day for the warrior to die. If he could reply yes, he was in a warrior state and ready to move forward without distractions.

### 7.   Do you have any requests?

This serves two purposes. First, essential matters that may need immediate attention can be addressed, making this the beginning of new coordination. Second, the new requests put you back in action with others, demonstrating that, no matter how bad it was, your common humanity allows you to take care of present concerns and prevent further deterioration and loss. In the two brothers' story, there were requests made about sharing information in customer files so business could continue.

**8.  Declare that the conflict is current in the moment and complete! You must say it!**

The declaration that the conflict is in the past serves a powerful purpose. You can now be present with each other in an opportunity to design the future. Of course, there will be a residual of past feelings, emotions, and beliefs that only time will quiet, but you have made the matter history by the power of your own intention and declaration. You have made a commitment to a more useful perspective.

**9.  What's the new era? The new era is _____.**

This gives you the opportunity to name the new era and declare what your future relationship will be. From a broad statement of intention about the nature of the new relationship come the specifics that go in your new agreement.

### Option Two—All Other Situations

This is a more businesslike way of asking questions very similar to those in Option One. The same explanatory notes apply.

1. What was effective about the original agreement? What worked?

2. What was ineffective? What didn't work?

3. What about your own behavior are you sorry for? (apology)

4. What can you say by way of compassion for the other participants' shortcomings or incompetence? (forgiveness)

5. What can you say by way of respect for the other people, their competence, their contribution, and their conduct in the situation? (thanks)

6. Pretending for a moment that you will never have another opportunity to speak about this matter, what else do you want to say?

7. Do you have any requests?

8. Declare completion!

9. What's the new era?

## The Completion Process at Work

During the process of completion, the two brothers opened a window to each other's heart and mind. Forgiveness and respect emerged. It was forged from airing the residue of what had broken down. That residue provided the raw material for the fabric of a new partnership. It was a different bond, forged and tempered from the heat of adversity and the cooling of catharsis and communication.

This is a sacred process. It is a great honor to be a guide and witness for people in relationships that have broken down. I am awed by what can emerge when people are committed enough to open their hearts, forgive, and let go of the past. Here are some stories that illustrate its effectiveness.

*Completion Within a Partnership.* Moriah and Bob were partners. They had pulled their consulting company up by the bootstraps. It was poised to move them into national recognition because of their innovative work in developing human potential. Their clients—individuals and companies—loved them and their work. But they were human! In their relationship, their personal psychological patterns were surfacing. They were resenting each other. They had stopped communicating. What seemed to be a great business marriage was turning into a nightmare. The atmosphere in their office was affecting their work, their income, and the future of their business.

They reached a point in their relationship where they had to clear the air—either move forward with a new level of understanding or separate their professional lives. They were familiar with the completion process. I suggested that they go off alone one afternoon and clear the air. Their conversation would not be easy—it called for hard work and emotional honesty. But through their tears they emerged as a stronger partnership. They learned they had the same vision for the future. They realized that what was setting them off was not what the other was doing but their reactions to their own ghosts from the past.

The courage to have a real-time conversation put their collaboration back on firm ground. They designed a new foundation for their working relationship based on current truth. They agreed to do a completion process every six months, no matter how well things were going. Today their partnership thrives. Each time they get complete, they free their creativity to go to the next level.

The breakdown of relationships that happened with Moriah and Bob occurs in all business and personal relationships. What we perceive in the external world is a reflection of all of our previous experiences. Often we are not aware of how much impact this has on our present reality. But our past is the source of most conflicts.

*Completion Within a High-Tech Company.* A few years ago, I introduced the "technology" of resolution to the executive committee of a growing technology company. The committee members were convinced that they could conserve a great deal of productive energy if they knew how to deal with conflict. The executives became fascinated with the entire process. They adopted the completion process as part of standard management practice. Now all teams, and every reporting relationship, come together four times a year to make sure nothing that could detract from productivity goes unsaid.

**Completion Within a Family.** Jerry and Lenore were locked in combat—to be right, to maintain control, to win, to get their way. Life was awful, even though they loved each other deeply. What unfolded was far better than the most riveting movie I have ever seen. I witnessed two people move from a great anger to great compassion. As they talked about what worked in their relationship, they realized the contribution they had made to each other. When they spoke of forgiveness, they forgave themselves for being angry and not seeing the way they had been jerks. Each forgave the other for their anger.

When they looked at thankfulness, they realized the value they had created—two great kids, a home, a circle of friends, and a business that employed 20 people. Their anger melted into love, and their fear turned to possibility as they decided to reinvent their relationship. Today they are thriving, both as a couple and as business partners. They emerged from the completion process with the ability to tap into the fun, humor, and creative genius that brought them together. They tapped the source of their original attraction.

**Completion Within My Family.** Last year, I decided to reframe my relationship with my parents. As is the nature of the parent/child relationship, I was carrying around the baggage of how my life was tarnished by their parenting. Mostly, they have been fine parents, always doing the best they could at the time. Going through the completion process was not easy, but it was very satisfying. It provided a sense of freedom most people don't get until their parents are gone. It completed the part of the parental relationship that locked me into the struggle that is part of parenting dynamics. It allowed a shift to a foundation based on common interests. I freed them of the need to be caretakers. I gained emotional autonomy.

## Summary

- Bringing everyone into the present moment is an essential component of resolution.

- The completion process ensures vulnerability about a situation.

- The structured conversation reveals feelings, empties emotional background, and moves you to stand in the other's shoes.

- Completion reveals the loss and the disappointment over expectations that are unrealized.

- Completion provides a context in which people grieve, let go of the past, and start designing the future.

## Reflections

- Practice the completion process three times: once with yourself about some part of your life you want to change; once with someone in your family; and once with someone at work.

- What was the value for you? For them?

- For the next three days, do completions about anything that troubles you.

- What has changed about your attitude?

# 19

# Reaching Agreement in Principle

If men would consider not so much wherein they differ, as wherein they agree, there would be far less of uncharitableness and angry feeling in the world.

*Joseph Addison*

It's happened hundreds of times. One side of the anticipated battle calls, fearing the worst—thinking of hiding assets, who will win, who will lose, and what will be the consequences of a battle. They are amazed to discover that, aside from the emotion of transition, the process can be relatively painless. Once you establish an agreement in principle, it can be easy.

By developing an agreement in principle, a

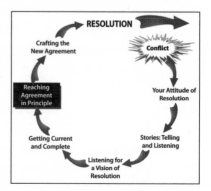

broad-brush understanding of the resolution, you sustain the momentum generated by the completion process.

Some questions for everyone to reflect on that will help sustain the movement toward an agreement are:

1. After the completion process, is the preliminary vision still on target?

2. How does the preliminary vision have to be modified to get to an agreement in principle?

3. Is the preliminary vision history? Do you have to start fresh, based on what has been articulated in the completion process?

This chapter discusses several techniques for answering these questions, which moves the process to an agreement in principle.

## What's the New Era?

The last question of the completion process is "What's the new era?" Although the energy may be heightened and the emotion raw, the response people give to this "innocent" question is a good barometer of what they want the future to be like. For example, if the new era in an employee dispute were to be a mentoring relationship, the agreement in principle is that the person would remain with the company. Their kneejerk response is a snapshot of their preferred future. Often it tells you exactly what the agreement in principle is. Sometimes you have more work to do.

## Trial Balloons

Telling the story and the completion process provide a clearer sense of where the situation is headed. Now you can send up some trial balloons to see if you have a foundation for a new agreement. After the completion process, generate a discussion by asking innocent questions about concerns like:

Companies—Are there business reasons for working together?

Colleagues—Will they continue working together?

Partnerships—Will we continue to be business partners?

Executives—Do they have a basis for a joint vision?

Litigation—Do we want to settle the claim or go to court?

Employment claims—Does an employee want to retain his or her job?

Divorce—Is there a desire for fighting or peaceful resolution?

A slight variation to using a trial balloon is making a suggestion. "What do you think about the idea of . . . " works well. It opens up the discussion. Others are free to pick it up, and the responses will give you ideas about where everyone is in the process. The opening gets everyone designing the solution.

### Small, Bite-Sized Chunks

Securing agreements in principle is best accomplished by taking small chunks within a context that "nothing is agreed until it is all agreed." Most people are less uptight about signing off on a particular concern if it is not written in stone. This provides leverage that can be used to bargain. In business disputes the keystone inquiry is whether, or how, people can continue working together. In a divorce, I like to establish early who will have child custody, a basic understanding about property division, and whether there will be a claim for alimony.

### Group Dynamics and Difficult People

As you move toward an agreement in principle, remember that people need to get comfortable working with each other in a new way. Folks have different levels of awareness and interpersonal and intra-personal skills that affect the group dynamics. Posturing may happen at the beginning. Even with good intentions and similar desired outcomes, group and personal dynamics are always part of the picture. People sometimes need to get beyond their insecurity and fear. You may need to air these feelings up front, rather than waiting until the agreement-in-principle step.

There will be difficult personalities. They will come in a variety of shapes and sizes. Stay aware of hostility and the forms in which it manifests: indecisiveness, complaining, negativism, silence, arrogance, and agreeableness. There is a body of knowledge and information for you to access in dealing with difficult facets of human personality.[30] Consult it when your common sense has not worked.

## The Irresistibility Principle

The irresistibility principle is a good way to get to an agreement in principle. In almost every conflict or new project, you can frame the desired outcome in a way that people in the situation will find irresistible—they have to say yes. A good illustration is the irresistible frame that my former wife placed around our divorce settlement. At the time this happened, we were both actively practicing lawyers. I was starting to get "lawyerlike" in the situation regarding our divorce settlement, and one day she called and said: "We have been through too much together, our friendship is too important, and to have anything but an honorable outcome would demean the marriage and our relationship. Let's agree that we will do this as friends, and preserve the dignity of what we have shared."

Light bulbs went off. It was irresistible to go for this result; on reflection, it was the obvious way to move forward. Taking that long view enabled us to create a deep friendship that has lasted for almost 30 years beyond our separation. Unfortunately, most people, because they have no model of a better way, choose to do battle.

The two brothers had two irresistible outcomes—brotherhood and no battle. Earlier in their conflict, no one had raised the concern of preserving family. Often the essential part of resolution is reframing the perceived problem into something else. Asking people to look back from their deathbed is a good way to get into the discussion. How would they like to see the situation resolved and how they would like to feel about themselves because of it. That is a very useful tool.

## Ongoing Feasibility Testing

Continuous feasibility testing is an important aspect of getting to resolution. Constantly check to see if everyone is engaged and on board. Poll for both major and minor objections. This keeps you on the path. Just keep asking!

## Many "Right Ways"

Are you concerned about making sure you do it right? You will! When you multiply the number of conflicts with the number of people who want an effective agreement, you have the number of right ways to accomplish this work. Being good at achieving desired outcomes is about having a positive intention and trusting your instincts. The right way is the way you sense will work. Often you just have to feel your way along. The conflict resolution model is the foundation from which you will develop your own artistry. You were born with most of the skills you need!

## Relief and Excitement

An important barometer in this step of the model is whether you are relieved and excited about reaching an agreement in principle. Moving from an agreement in principle to a complete agreement is more businesslike than the emotionally taxing work leading up to it. The key hurdle is getting an agreement in principle after doing the deeper emotional work. When you have a basic agreement, you can breathe more easily. You are now on the same team. This is what the completion process is designed to accomplish.

It's a joy to observe the achievement of an agreement in principle. People realize they will not have to fight. I have seen the tension leave the faces of joint venture partners, business partners, unhappy consumers, fighting spouses, battling neighbors, executive teams, and companies and their employees. It confirms that even though we have trained and girded ourselves for battle, we don't want to fight.

### *Summary*

- An agreement in principle is an elegant way to turn the corner and a big step toward reaching agreement.

- It's like being at the top of a ski run. From there you slide to the bottom, but you must steer along the way.

- The key is reaching agreement on a big picture understanding of what the future will look like, and naming that the "new era."

### *Reflections*

- Practice the irresistibility principle by looking at a few situations you see as difficult.

- What suggestion can you make that everyone, including yourself, will say yes to?

- Introduce what you think will be irresistible by asking, "What do you think about . . . ?"

# 20

STEP 6
## Crafting the
## New Agreement

> Covenantal relationships induce freedom not paralysis. A covenantal relationship rests on shared commitment to ideas, to issues, to values, to goals. . . . Words such as love, warmth, personal chemistry are certainly pertinent. Covenantal relationships are open to influence.
>
> *Max DePree,* Leadership Is an Art [31]

Resolution is present when you have a shared vision for the future. What was intolerable becomes history. Because the conflict is no longer present in your life, you no longer think about it. In the agreement step of the resolution model, you articulate the innovative solutions that you and the others in the conflict invent together. It puts

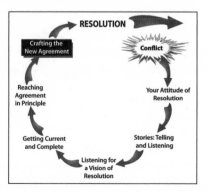

the detail on the bones of the agreement in principle/new era. In the process, this creates trust that eliminates conflict or, in the case of a new relationship, facilitates starting on a solid foundation. How to express a clear covenantal agreement for results —the sixth step of the resolution model—is the subject of this chapter.

## The Power of Agreement

When you think about agreements, you probably think of difficult negotiations and long legal documents. You focus on protecting yourself from the what-ifs of the situation. A more useful way to define *agreement* is as: (1) a joint vision; (2) the product of an effective conflict resolution process; or (3) the foundation for a successful new team, partnership, or relationship. This definition is true for your business or domestic partner, spouse, family members, colleagues, work teams, or joint venturers, or for your company and its employees or customers.

Agreements define how you coordinate the activities of people working together—how they collaborate—and collaboration is the foundation of any accomplishment! Successful collaboration is like dancing, but often you have different ideas about the steps in the dance. These differences can lead to greater synergy or to breakdown. Creating synergy and excellent results depend on clear agreements. Effective agreements express joint vision and provide a road map for producing results. The art of crafting effective agreements increases the likelihood of obtaining desired outcomes.

| THE BAD NEWS | THE GOOD NEWS |
|---|---|
| *You were not taught to craft effective agreements. It was not part of your core educational curriculum.* | *You can learn!* |

## The Law and Principles of Agreement: Why Agreements Are Important

The following law and principles of agreement explain in a linear way why agreements are so fundamental to work and to life and why they are the foundation for coordination, the essence of productivity.

### *The Law of Agreement*

1. The source of productivity and fulfillment in any relationship is effective collaboration. The tighter the collaboration, the better the results.

### *The Principles of Agreement*

2. You collaborate in language by making implicit agreements (talking to yourself about what you think the agreement is) and explicit agreements (discussing the agreement with others).

3. You work and live in a sea of agreements.

4. You never learned the essential elements of an effective agreement.

5. Clear agreements express shared vision and how to get there. Clear agreements empower and contribute to desired results.

6. Clear agreements improve the chances for satisfaction. They set up the conditions that produce delighted clients, customers, teammates, colleagues, vendors, and family members.

7. Practice enables you to craft masterful agreements.

8. No matter how clear and complete the agreement, everything will not be addressed—conflicts and differences will arise.

9. Breakdowns are not a cause for alarm, they are to be expected. Breakdowns are an opportunity for creativity.

10. Resolving conflicts leads to new agreements.

## Mastering the Art of Agreement

The following Ten Essential Elements are the items that must be discussed if you want to create a vision and a map for getting the results you want. I have compared the mind-set of an Agreements for Results perspective, with the traditional agreements-for-protection mental model. The essence of Agreement for Results is that we get into conflict because we never learned how to craft explicit agreements that create a meeting of mind and heart. The best way to prevent conflict and to have more productive and satisfying relationships is to begin all collaborations with an Agreement for Results on the front end.

### *The Ten Essential Elements are:*

1. **Intent and vision.** Big picture of what you want. The clearer and more specific the desired outcomes, the more likely you will succeed as visualized.

2. **Roles**. The duties, responsibilities, and commitment of everyone you need to achieve the desired results.

3. **Promises**. Promises of action steps. Specific commitments tell you if the actions will get you to the desired results.

4. **Time and value.** All promises have "by whens," the time the agreement will become effective. Is the exchange fair and does it provide enough incentive?

5. **Measurements of satisfaction.** The evidence that you achieved your objectives must be clear, direct, and measurable to eliminate conflict about whether you accomplished what you set out to do.

6. **Concerns and fears.** Unspoken difficulties need to be expressed, and the fear behind them addressed. This deepens understanding of what you are taking on, and the partnership you are creating with yourself.

7. **Renegotiation.** No matter how optimistic and clear, it will become necessary to renegotiate promises and conditions of satisfaction because things change. The *quality* of working relationships is more important than anything.

8. **Consequences.** Know the consequences for breaking promises, and what will be lost to the parties, the organizations and the public if the project is not completed.

9. **Conflict resolution.** Conflicts and disagreements *will* arise. Agree to an attitude of resolution, with an agreed resolution process.

10. **Agreement?** When you have reflected on 1–9, ask whether you trust moving forward. Do not move into action until all can say yes, then commit to embrace the future as an opportunity to be enjoyed.

The model draws out both the vision, and the road map to it. It provides a path to what you want to accomplish. For example, making an agreement with your new client is an excellent way of framing the relationship!

## Results v. Protection Compared

|  | Results focus | Protection focus |
| --- | --- | --- |
| Intent and vision | Desired outcome | What ifs |
| Roles | Take responsibility | Limit accountability |
| Promises | Commitment | Qualifiers and conditioners |
| Time and value | By whens/fair return | Most for least |
| Measurements of satisfaction | Inspiring goals | Excuses and escapes |
| Concerns and fears | Compassion/understanding | Edge for strategic advantage |
| Renegotiation | Deal with unknowns/changes | Strike hard bargain |
| Consequences | Reminder of promises | Punishment |
| Conflict resolution | Get back on track | Exact some premium |
| Agreement ? | Trust enough | Escape possible? |

## Three Phases of Agreement

As you learn to work with the elements of agreements, remember these three distinct phases:

1. *The process of agreement.* This is the series of conversations in which you talk about each of the elements. Following the process enables you to determine if shared vision and trust are present. If so, you can declare that you have an agreement.

2. *The phenomenon of agreement.* When you have completed the agreement process, you should have a shared vision. If you do, hearts and minds are together in a covenantal relationship focused on producing a certain result. If this phenomenon of agreement is present, you have an agreement that you can trust. If you do not trust that this phenomenon is present, you are not ready to move forward with the relationship.

3. *The artifact of agreement.* When you have the phenomenon of agreement, the essence of the covenant

should be put in writing. This will act as a guide as you
move forward with the relationship.

## Agreements in Lieu of Conflict

The two brothers are a classic example of how the process
works. When they came to a resolution, an agreement was
crafted that expressed a new working relationship: Tom would
own the existing business, and he would pay Bill for his share of
that business; Bill would have exclusive rights to a geographical area in which to operate his new business; and they would
help and advise each other so each could benefit from the experience of the other. They let go of their acute discomfort and
pain. Each stepped into the new context that each had articulated for his future, demonstrating that the real resolution of
conflict is a new agreement for the future.

A resolution between IBM and Fujitsu demonstrates how
creativity can produce new value where others see conflict. Fujitsu had developed a computer operating system for IBM that
IBM wanted to use in certain applications. A dispute developed
about ownership rights. Because of the possibility for thousands
of individual lawsuits, litigation had the potential to keep an
army of lawyers busy for decades. An agreement was reached
that provided for preservation of the relationship through a series of cross-licensing agreements. Instead of acrimony, both
companies earned millions from their new agreement.

In another resolution, a bankrupt manufacturer who
owed over $1 million to a former supplier induced the sup-
plier to continue business in the future; in a new agreement,
the manufacturer paid a premium on future supplies to cover
the past debt. It enabled the supplier to get whole eventually, and the manufacturer to emerge from bankruptcy, regain
viability, and save the jobs of thousands of employees.

New agreements are especially important for divorces that involve children. It is fortunate when parents understand that co-parenting gives children the benefit of two parents and that children will be harmed if acrimony continues. Working out the details of co-parenting is the first step in a new form of collaboration.

If you can fully step into a new way of thinking, you will no longer have to "process" the conflict. You will not be concerned about fixing blame, inducing guilt, or being right. You will not have to suffer. You will realize that joy and productivity comes from coordinating with others and that the dance of agreement is the edge where life is rich and exciting. You want to be back in action quickly. Just put in place new agreements and move forward. The conflict will be in the past, superseded by the new agreement. That is my vision.

Agreement making is a practice that can be learned and mastered. Try it! I guarantee your results will improve.

### Summary

- Crafting effective agreements is an elegant way of arriving at a shared vision for the future, either as the final step of resolving conflict or as the initial step at the beginning of a new project, transaction, or relationship.

- It is an essential skill that you never learned.

- The laws of agreement provide a simple logic that demonstrates the value of agreement in any situation.

- The Ten Essential Elements are:
  1. Intent and Vision
  2. Roles
  3. Promises

4. Time Value

5. Measurements of Satisfaction

6. Concerns and Fears

7. Renegotiation

8. Consequences

9. Conflict Resolution

10. Agreement?

- By using the elements of agreement you achieve the "phenomenon" of agreement, a relationship based on covenant.

## *Reflections*

- Choose someone you admire, someone with whom you want to work on a project.

- Approach the person and, using the agreement template, craft an agreement about the project.

- Try it at home—work out an agreement about an area that has been troublesome, and watch the conflict fade into history.

- Results? Reactions?

# 21

# Resolution

## Resolution Is . . .

Resolution is an outcome.

Resolution is the condition of everyone and each one's resources after a conflict, dispute, disagreement, or breakdown is put to rest.

Resolution induces everyone to address his or her relationships.

Resolution returns everyone to productivity and coordination.

Resolution requires:

- Moving from conflict to a workable agreement, a dynamic context for action and cooperation.

- Honoring everyone's concerns.

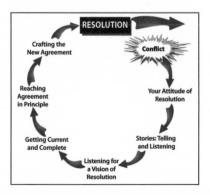

- Taking actions that put the conflict and its impact to rest.
- Committing to ongoing relationships.
- Getting beyond everyone's emotional positions.
- Establishing a vision for the future that lets go of blame, punishment, and damages and recognizes others' value.
- Recognizing new practices essential for the success of ongoing relationships.
- Being willing to learn, having the courage to change, and the compassion to forgive.

Masterful resolution requires that all involved say:

- They have won.
- Their resources have been optimized by the process.
- Although conflict and breakdowns are inevitable in life, they are in better condition to handle them in the future.

This chapter discusses how to manifest the vision the resolution embodies.

## Resolution Gives Life

Gail Johnson is the executive director of Sierra Adoption, a nonprofit organization transforming lives of foster children through finding permanent adoptive families. Thousands of children are trapped in the California foster care system, out of reach of adoptive families. More than half of foster youth who come of age without a permanent family are homeless, in prison, or dead within two years. Early on, Gail's efforts at recruiting and preparing families to adopt children with disabilities often ended in the frustration of being told such children were "unadoptable." Because of Gail's work, California no longer considers any child unadoptable!

In 1999 Sierra was engaged in a federally funded partnership with the Sacramento County agency that was referring children to Sierra. The working relationship had fallen apart. Gail wanted to resolve long- and short-term conflict, get beyond mistrust, and forge a high-performance team. Few believed the partnership could even be salvaged. Sixteen people were gathered and over two days and, using the Cycle of Resolution, the conflicts were resolved and a working agreement structured. That agreement was the foundation for a healthy, productive partnership with a new vision of collaboration. In the first year following the intervention, 109 "unadoptable" children were placed in permanent families.

## Manifesting Your Desired Results

Scientists in quantum physics labs have observed that certain subatomic particles exist only when they are observed. You might conclude that the power of observation, the focused attention of the conscious mind, has the power to create matter in the physical universe. Do we all have the power to think things into existence? This phenomenon is mentioned in the books of the best-selling author and physician Deepak Chopra.[32]

A correlate of this premise is that, when you have a clear picture of what you desire in the future, the resources needed to realize the vision will be attracted to the situation by the power of your subconscious mind. This has been explained by Napoleon Hill in the classic *Think and Grow Rich*[33] and by Maxwell Maltz in *Psycho-Cybernetics*.[34]

Every principle, practice, model, and story in this book has one central purpose: freeing you to have the results and fulfillment you want with the least struggle and the most elegant use of resources. This is called manifestation.

## The Laws of Manifestation

The following is a linear expression of the best way to manifest your vision:

1. Thoughts manifest themselves in physical form.

2. Consciously and habitually feed your mind thoughts that express the reality in which you want to live.

3. Express your vision in your thoughts.

4. Be very specific in your vision of the future.

5. Agreements are powerful tools of manifestation, expressing joint vision, producing synergy, and increasing value.

6. Agreements help produce satisfaction and material desires.

7. Consciousness about our thoughts makes us human.

8. You can choose what you think!

9. See Law 1!

## Resolution Is Leadership

A few years ago I asked nationally known leadership expert Jim Kouzes[35] "When do leaders give up, change directions, or realize they have been barking up the wrong tree?" Without hesitation he said, "They don't. They don't blame others, they don't make excuses for poor performance, they don't quit. Once they decide on a course of action, they just keep moving forward, making corrections as they go along, but not turning back."

This same tenacity gets you to resolution because resolution embodies the same competencies and behaviors essential for effective leadership. You must understand, honor, and be thankful for the differing values and realities that everyone brings to a situation. You give yourself the authority to resolve things so that action and productivity will proceed. You continually define ambiguity as a situation unfolds so that you form a context of relative certainty. You develop a compelling vision for the future that gives purpose and meaning to the tasks of others. Acting like a resolutionary contributes to your personal identity as a leader. It will be recognized by people working with you because it is a hallmark of leadership.

## *Summary*

- Physical reality is shaped by your thoughts. Combining your thoughts with those of others to produce shared vision is a powerful leadership tool that contributes to producing the outcomes you want.

- This is achieved through the power and principles of manifestation and resolution.

- At the end of a conflict, or the beginning of a new project, there is great power in the resolution that a clear, shared agreement has produced.

- Leadership is taking responsibility for making things happen in the world, and the same characteristics that make excellent leaders make excellent resolutionaries.

## *Reflections*

- Think about something you have been wanting in your life.

- Choose someone to partner with in making it happen.

- Craft an agreement with that person. Notice the resources that arrive to support your vision.

- Do this at work and at home.

# 22

## Applying the Principles: The Craft of Resolution

If we work in marble, it will perish; if we work upon brass, time will efface it; if we rear temples, they will crumble into dust; but if we work upon immortal minds and instill into them just principles, we are then engraving upon tablets which no time will efface, but will brighten and brighten to all eternity.

*Daniel Webster*

Following a model to resolve conflicts and construct agreements for your projects, transactions, and relationships seems like a stretch because we are reluctant to talk in a linear way about things that we believe exist in a more emotional realm. This reaction reflects our habits of thinking. Many of us think of conflict as a "life force," and are afraid that eliminating the drama of conflict will diminish what drives us and makes us feel alive.

I am not suggesting eliminating differences, only offering a new way of dealing with them—developing a new habit. Having disagreements and differences adds vibrancy, creativity, and innovation to life, but ongoing hostile conflict does not. Using the model will quiet your internal chatter and provide the freedom to be more productive in the present moment. Conflict and differences will not disappear, but you will develop the capacity to respond more productively.

Using the Cycle of Resolution model can become an effective new habit because, like a road map, it tells you exactly where to go—something that is especially important when you are going somewhere for the first time. It prescribes a series of steps that require using the principles of the new paradigm. To make clear how the principles and model connect, this chapter explains how the model serves each of the ten principles.

## The Ten Principles as Applied to the Model

### Abundance

This principle permeates everything. The model demands believing that there is enough for everyone to be satisfied. The principle of abundance is thus a foundation of the model.

### Efficiency

The model takes the guesswork and wasted energy out of forming effective agreements and resolving conflict quickly. It provides a map that helps you:

1. Decide if you have a workable agreement.
2. Maximize the potential for success by creating a shared vision.
3. Minimize conflict due to misunderstanding.
4. Deal with conflict directly, at its core.

Chapter 20 discussed the key elements of effective agreements. The following discussion shows how these elements contribute to the efficient use of resources.

*Intent and Specific Vision.* With intent and a specific vision, you quickly begin thinking about the result you want—the big picture of the resolution or collaboration, as well as a specific picture of what you want to create together. You quickly see if everyone has the same vision.

*Roles and Promises.* When roles and promises are articulated, you know at an early stage whether these roles and promises are enough to manifest the vision, whether other people need to be brought in, and whether you can embrace your role.

*Measurements of Satisfaction.* If you state up front how the outcome will be measured, there is little wasted energy discussing whether you achieved your purpose. It is a yes/no observation—either you did it, or not!

*Concerns and Fears.* Concerns and fears are a huge drag on productivity, and speaking about them efficiently gets rid of this heavy baggage.

*Renegotiation, Dissolution, and Dispute Resolution.* Setting up a process on the front end for resolving inevitable conflict saves a great deal of emotional energy when these situations occur, and it contributes to developing the attitude of resolution.

### Creativity

Creativity involves two important aspects. The first is emotional. Where conflict exists, fear is present, and fear is a great impediment to creativity. By promoting resolution, the model also promotes creativity. The other aspect is the value of structure. A model provides a framework within which you know and trust that the process will take care of the required elements; you won't miss anything. This gives you the freedom to be creative.

### Fostering Resolution

Three elements of our present system guarantee conflict: (1) the adversary mind-set generated by fear of losing or being exploited, (2) the paradigm of cutting off communication once conflict occurs, and (3) the game-like sport of win or lose that we often take for granted.

Following the model eliminates these practices. The attitude of resolution recognizes that everyone loses when people respond to conflict in an adversarial way. The model is designed to get to resolution quickly and use conflict creatively. The model demands engagement and dialogue, which fosters productivity. Knowing that the process holds the potential for everyone to win takes away the jousting that is currently so prevalent.

### Openness

The model requires you to be open and authentic. The steps to resolution are designed to help you disclose your observations, reveal your feelings, understanding the grief arising from the disappointed expectation, and stand in the shoes of the other side. This requires authentic self-revelation. Revealing what the model requires—thankfulness, forgiveness, apology, and fears—demands vulnerability. The benefit is that agreements are formed, and transactions take place, much closer to people's core. The closer to bedrock the personal commitment is, the greater the potential result. You develop "relationships based on covenant."[36]

### Long-Term Collaborations

The agreement template builds long-term partnership. If you take the time to engage in conversations covering the elements of the agreement, you are serious about building something that will last.

The model is designed to articulate the joint vision. It is intended for people who are concerned about producing results and effective collaboration. Taking time to articulate a vision that incorporates the desires of all people involved is not a casual matter. Clearly expressing conditions of satisfaction provides long-term goals for the collaboration.

### Feelings and Intuition

Using the model requires going beyond the rational and the linear. In going through the elements of agreement, you realize that the phenomenon or covenant of agreement exists—your heart says yes. The yes comes from your entire self, not just your logic. It is much more than an intellectual exercise. Sharing fears demands attention to your emotions. So does grieving, as well as expressing thankfulness and forgiveness. The entire experience takes you beyond the left brain.

### Full Disclosure

Following the model requires complete disclosure—at the beginning, when the relationship is first established, and as an ongoing commitment to keep the relationship clean (no internal chatter). When secrets are eliminated, the energy wasted on keeping them is available for productivity. You never have to worry about what you are hiding because nothing is hidden.

### Learning

When you are resolving a conflict or structuring a new project, you are learning your way to the desired result. First, you listen and learn what others need. Then, you learn what you need. Finally, together, you learn your way to the agreement that will satisfy everyone. A mind-set of inquiry rather than of "knowing" makes resolution possible.

### ResponseAbility

You cannot leave it to a professional. You cannot hide behind a process that requires less than authenticity, engagement, and full participation. No one can participate in the practices of the model for you. You must be present in the agreement making discussions. You must decide if this is a person you want to engage and work with, a person whom you trust to work through inevitable conflicts with you.

### Summary

- The principles are the foundation on which the model is based. Understanding how the model serves the principles will help motivate you to honor the principles and use the model.

### *Reflections*

- It takes approximately 21 days of repetition to "install" a new habit. So please either photocopy the list of principles or copy the principles on an index card.

- Carry the card with you and for the next 21 days, and before you sit down to eat a meal, review and reflect on them. Do not spend more than three minutes.

- The learning process will be helped if you share what you are doing with others.

# 23

# Benefits and Utility: The Cycle of Resolution

Nothing in this world is so good as usefulness.

*B.C. Forbes*

You will find that the model is useful in all areas of your life. Remember, it's not brilliant insights that catalyze improvement; it's consistent application of simple principles. As you go through this chapter, please think about ways that using the model might improve areas of your life.

## The Power of Agreement and Resolution

Beginning with or getting to a solid agreement embodies a clearly defined, shared vision of the future. It fuels productive energy forward, toward creating—manifesting—that vision in the physical world. The vision is the starting point of the creation.

The extraordinary freeing of energy that takes place when people realize they can put down their guns, take a deep breath, and get back to their productive lives is amazing to behold. Resolution confirms the human inclination to nurture, love, and take care of each other. This principle was illustrated by Chilean biologist and writer Humberto Maturana, who points out that the human hand is constructed in a way that is uniquely capable of caressing any part of the body. If you doubt the premise, imagine caressing someone with a hoof or a claw.[37]

I repeatedly observe the phenomenon of nurturance with business partners, executives, divorcing couples, and collaborators of all kinds. When the completion process is finished, the cobwebs are cleared. The individuals remember their attraction and harmony and can start working on an agreement as partners; they finish it in a fraction of the time expected, with joy and emotional release instead of pain. The weight of preoccupation holding down their productivity, growth, and the rest of their life is released. People have told me that it feels as if their wings have been restored. They feel light and unbridled, free again to soar. They expected a long, contentious, painful process. They did not believe resolution was possible.

The vice-president of marketing for a large manufacturing company was being "restructured" out of a merged organization. Even though he was not unhappy with his severance package, he was ready to fight for more. This stance was based more on what well-meaning friends were saying he was entitled to than on what *he* wanted. Rather than asking for a lot and getting involved in an extended conflict, he asked for a few things, which were granted, and he was elated. He could now turn to face the rest of his life. He did not have to fight about something in the past. His energy and creativity were free to devote to a new plan. This phenomenon was present for the two brothers from Chapter 3. Instead of a battle, they were building new businesses.

Imagine what the Hatfields and McCoys might have produced if they weren't always engaged in a battle. The same is true for the Israelis and Palestinians. The habit of "having an enemy" keeps you wasting precious life force in fighting. The battles evidence fear: fear of an unknown future, of a new order of things, of a new life force without an enemy to battle. You are holding onto an old structure because of the fear of not knowing what the new structure will be. You don't realize that you hold the power to make up the new structure. You can construct a future using the tool of agreement. This new agreement will be the new structure, although it is one you are not ready to trust. You have to learn that usually there is no enemy if you don't create one.

### *Incremental Power*

There is great power in the resolution of joining your vision with others. The synergy of teamwork is extraordinary. Simple proof are the powerful Clydesdale horses that pull the Budweiser wagon. One Clydesdale can pull 7,000 pounds; two can pull between 18,000 and 25,000 pounds! At a time when we all are being asked to produce more with less, we need greater incremental performance (accomplishing more with less) both at home and at work.

At work you are facing downsizing, rightsizing, reengineering, layoffs, and mergers. At home you feel increasing demands for personal growth; self-actualization; and being better parents, siblings, spouses, children, producers, or performers. It is challenging to feel adequate. The weight on your shoulders is dizzying. Each day you see the fissures in the armor of the rugged-individual, Marlboro-man philosophy that built the United States. How can you accomplish more with less?

Tight coordination and a shared vision allow the miracles of teamwork and collaboration to occur. Clear agreement with others builds teams that can experience an exponential expansion of power. In times of economic downturn, the collaborative leverage that clear agreements brings can be the difference between a successful and a failed enterprise.

## Agreements at Work

Business is the central focus of capitalist society. It is a place where you participate as owner, boss, employee, and consumer. As you work with others in pursuit of common goals, opportunity abounds for resolving conflict and reaching clear agreements. For example, agreements by senior executive teams create joint vision for the direction of an organization. They define roles, responsibilities, tasks, and how results are to be measured. The conversations leading to the agreement, and the action in pursuit of agreed-upon goals, creates covenant and collaboration. Companies waste energy as internal chatter clutters productive capacity. But when the model is followed nothing is left unsaid. Get rid of chatter and you double your output.

Following are specific ways that clear agreements help at work:

*Conflict Resolution.* A conflict resolution process provides the peace of knowing that a path to resolution has been established. People can invent a new framework for their future. Nonadversarial ways of bringing closure to emotional relationships leave fewer scars and better soil for new beginnings with people you must work with.

*Joint Ventures and Mergers.* The level of success increases because detailed joint vision is articulated. Increasingly, business alliances with other organizations are used to build "virtual organizations." Agreements are also successful in incorporating departments of different companies into effective operational units.

*Employment Relationships.* Steven Covey says that to have empowered employees you need trust, and to achieve trust you need performance agreements.[38] The agreement spells out desired results, guidelines, accountability, and consequences. In effect, employees design their jobs. When people participate in shaping and customizing their working relationships, productivity leaps take place because the participants are inspired and motivated by the objectives and standards that they shaped. Mutuality is fostered, resentment is eliminated, and acceptance is assured.

*Teams.* Managers, department heads, and team leaders can use agreements to keep their units on the same track. Articulating a shared vision and establishing clear conditions of satisfaction are crucial to this task. They operate both within and between departments and companies. This is true for virtual and self-directed teams, increasingly the backbone of business organizations. As you ask for increased participation and self-management, you must provide the tools that optimize team resources and keep everyone on track. Agreements, and the means to establish and revise them, are very useful, sorely needed tools. There are dozens of situations where team agreements are the "bible" used to evaluate performance and results and to provide direction and guidance in implementing the organizational mission and specific team objectives.

*Mood and Attitude.* When you are engaged in designing the specifics of your participation, you are a willing player—less resentful, happier, and more engaged.

*Productivity of Work Groups.* The work becomes primary, not the politics of relationships. Joint vision and the tactical moves to achieve objectives become the focus. Internal chatter is quieted.

*Creativity and Innovation.* The absence of hostile conflict enables clear thinking, which is essential to doing tasks more efficiently. The energy that was locked in conflict is available for creativity.

*Consultants, Professionals, Vendors, and Salespeople.* There is greater ability to build relationships that increase the potential of satisfying customers by crafting clear agreements that (1) establish a joint vision of desired results, and (2) specify how the satisfaction of expectations will be measured. Clear agreements make all vendors and service providers an integral part of the team because everyone understands their contribution to profitability and the satisfaction of the final consumer.

*Customer/Client Satisfaction.* When you are clear about tasks and free of chatter, you can concentrate on the customer.

*Labor Relations.* Unions become part of the team—partners in producing results, part of the virtual organization.

*Legal Agreements.* Lawyers can craft agreements that focus as much on achieving results as on protecting clients from problems.

*Lawsuits.* An early process that fosters resolution prevents situations from getting out of hand.

*Diversity Issues.* People see how they are the same and that they want the same things. Differences are acknowledged in the process of crafting agreements. As individual concerns are expressed and heard, people are "legitimized." Groups get the benefit of individual genius.

I consulted with a start-up technology company that was developing a new telecommunications application. The company had been stuck for six months. Marketing and product development were battling over ready dates, finance was breathing down everyone's neck, and the venture capitalists hovered over everything. In one day, we broke through and jump-started the operation. Developing clear promises of action and a joint mission got everyone moving.

As companies are globalized and flattened and new principles of management pervade, there must be a vehicle that people use to accomplish the work of the organization. The Model of Resolution can be that vehicle! [39]

## Agreements at Home

You don't think of having specific behavioral agreements with spouses, children, friends, or family members. I suggest they might be of great benefit. My experience is that agreements defining relationships can produce the quality we want in these personal situations and can help us reduce the sources of friction.

In marriages and other intimate relationships, agreements can reflect unique individual realities. You can agree about areas of permanent concern, such as relatives, social life, money, and career. Spouses can articulate what they want and need in their relationship. Family members can define what "family" means to them. Couples about to marry can design a customized foundation for the future.

There is as much value in the conversations that lead to the agreement as in the agreement itself. The model provides the structure for the conversations that explore individual thinking about a particular subject. It is a tool for deepening relationships and providing guidelines for behavior. Updating the agreement keeps relationships fresh and shifts difficulties from defensive explanations about behavior to those that are practical and behavioral. The model provides a means of resolving conflict without the need of outside help.

I used the model in a long-term relationship. My partner and I jointly produced a vision for the relationship we wanted. It expressed our separate visions for the future and the vision we had of what the relationship would be. We made promises to each other about how we would act as a couple and how we would structure our lives. We placed a time limit on the agreement and had a structure for renegotiating our promises. We included standards for the following areas of our life:[40]

Physical Fitness

Finances

Play Time

Membership

Social Life

Personal Dignity

Family

Planetary Concerns

Work

Spirituality

Education

Career

The conversations that led to our agreements were extraordinary. Writing the agreement was an exhilarating exercise of joint creation, much more profound and stretching than either of us imagined. The agreement was a heroic document whose words were a powerful, inspiring force.

After five years we realized that we were not being served by staying together. Although separating was emotionally difficult, it was a smooth and orderly transition. The decision to separate, although painful, was not hard to make. When we evaluated the results that we had produced against the standards that we agreed on, it provided a clear answer about what we had to do.

As I look back, I am grateful for the experience. The inspiration and motivation provided by both going through the process leading to the agreement and living within the structure of the agreement were profound. The agreement was a catalyst for many of my accomplishments. It provided a foundation for the relationship, a foundation I jointly designed. It was a personal banner far more empowering than implicitly adopting standards and norms that are accepted as part of our culture, which is what most people do when they get married.

A few years ago I was asked to help a family with a rebellious 14-year-old. I had never used the model in this kind of situation, but I saw no reason that it wouldn't work.

John was having difficulty in almost every area of his life. His grades were below expectations, threatening his ability to get into college. He was abusing alcohol and drugs. He was not showing up for school. He fought with his parents every day. Previous interventions included counseling with the school psychologist, private counseling, special summer camp, and every kind of punishment you can imagine. These were all attempts to fix someone who was not broken.

I invited the family for a session. The key to making the session effective was getting John to believe that he would be listened to without interruption, that he would be heard, and that his feelings and vision would be considered in the resolution. Once he believed that and he felt free to communicate, the process was not difficult. John opened with his anger and resentment about always being compared to his sister, who was seven years older. She was one of those perfect kids—straight As, prom queen, president of her class.

John didn't want to be his sister. He never felt "heard" in his desire to pursue theater and the arts. As long as his talents were not recognized, he would continue being defiant. It was his way of getting attention.

I asked John to articulate how he wanted to be treated and why. His parents were amazed at how thoughtful he was. Together they crafted an agreement that provided detailed guidance about his education, contributions to the household, ability to make decisions for himself, and choice of friends.

John completed high school and started taking art courses. He enrolled in the junior college while working as a draftsman for a local architect. He finished junior college near the top of his class, transferred, and will soon receive a degree in architecture. The key was legitimizing him by listening, and empowering him to participate in making up his future.

## Agreements in Your Communities

Agreements can be used for mapping the direction and purpose of any organization. A few years ago, I was active with a self-appointed civic group that took up the banner of "reinventing" local government.

We used the agreement model to chart a course of action. The purpose of our group was to eliminate duplication of services among police, fire, road, vehicle maintenance, and parks and recreation that were provided by municipalities, utilities, and county government, as well as to take advantage of economies of scale. We developed a vision of the desired result. It included a political referendum to fold all of the municipalities into one county government with continued representation from the formerly independent entities. This would eliminate waste and inefficiency.

Our agreement included a plan for gathering information, projecting potential savings, garnering political support, dealing with resistance, and engaging in political action. We made promises about what we would do. We had a series of expectations with time frames to let us know if we were reaching our objectives. We determined how to resolve conflict and who would be responsible for making sure that we were on track. Even though everyone wanted to move immediately into action, the upfront planning was worth the effort. It produced commitment.

Agreements can get to the real task instead of dissipating resources in an adversarial political process. About 20 years ago a community group was formed to build a school for autistic children. The school served as a statewide model for other local groups that were concerned with the same problem. To me, it is a classic example, worth telling here, of what coordinated action driven by passionate concern can produce.

**School for Autistic Children.** When my law partner introduced me to the situation, the community group wanted to file a lawsuit against the federal, state, county, and local governments and their educational and mental health agencies. The group consisted of the parents of 22 autistic children of varying ages. These children had slipped through the cracks of various federal and state laws; the bottom line was that no one would take responsibility for educating the children.

I suggested a slightly different tack. I met with the parents to determine what they really wanted. Predictably, their concern was giving their kids the best education possible, given current understandings about dealing with autism. They believed starting a school was best. The kids were not mentally ill but severely emotionally compromised. We mapped out a short-term strategy for getting funds for the coming school year until a longer term resolution was put in place.

We had two strategies: (1) a legislative and fundraising agenda, and (2) starting a school. The parents were as committed and dedicated a group as I have ever worked with. Given the PR potential, their cause fell on receptive political ears, and they received approval and funding for a new school. Three years after that initial meeting, other school districts from the state were sending students to the school. This school was the first of a number that were funded around the state. That part of the story provides small gratification compared with the more important result. The dedicated school staff, along with outside experts, developed a program that was returning kids to the public schools. This was a result that was way beyond expectation.

Given the need for more efficiency in government, the vehicle of agreement is a natural. As part of Vice President Gore's "reinventing government" program, I reviewed agreements between President Clinton and the cabinet secretaries, defining specific objectives for essential government departments. Although much more detail could be placed in the documents, it was evident that senior administration officials had embraced the idea of using agreements as a way to get things done. Bravo!

## Agreements With Yourself

The model can be used to resolve intrapersonal conflicts or for planning—making agreements with yourself that chart a new course of action for your future.

***George and Marsha.*** George was having great difficulty with his ex-wife Marsha. There was ongoing conflict surrounding their joint custody agreement. They had been through years of counseling before their divorce. They had been in and out of court and had spent thousands on legal fees. Finally, George realized he was a big part of the problem because he automatically reacted to the position Marsha took; whatever Marsha said, George said the opposite. I had a sense that if he sat down with the agreement template and made all the decisions without the input of others, it would help get him to the bottom of things. Shortly thereafter, when his pain was so great because he was afraid he might lose the joint custody arrangement if he couldn't learn how to manage himself, George sat down in the privacy of his room. Alone, he saw the whole situation. He realized that a new agreement with himself about his behavior (the only thing he could control) might be the end of the war with Marsha.

George's vision was their ability to have calm and purposeful parenting discussions in which he listened and tried to understand her motivations. He wanted his child to have the benefit of a co-parenting relationship. Discussions might then lead to consensus that incorporated their joint wisdom.

He made these promises to himself:

1. To listen to her

2. To keep his tone conversational when speaking

3. To take classes in communication skills

4. To tell her when he was losing control so they could take a time out

5. To apologize whenever he "lost it"

6. To penalize himself $100 when he broke his promises

To measure whether he had met the agreement, he set a condition: going one full year without arguing with Marsha or calling his attorney. He acknowledged that no matter how resolute he felt now, he might not be able to pull it off.

But George was able to keep the agreement because it was voluntary; he had a different attitude than when his ex-wife, his lawyer, his therapist, or a judge told him what his agreement would be. At the end of the year, he was thankful, especially because of the long-term impact on his son, Peter. Instead of living in the emotional tug of war between his parents, Peter is becoming the product of their combined wisdom.

You can use the agreement model to plan objectives and help get what you want. I use the model for setting goals about writing, income, and physical exercise. It works! Something happens when you exercise the discipline of crafting an agreement with yourself. Getting specific about your goals is a form of creative visualization. Anyone in the business of goal-setting will tell you that it is essential to write down your goals. Making an agreement with yourself is another form of doing that.

### Summary

- Having agreements for all aspects of our life seems radical; however, the effect is worth it when you examine the results produced in business, community, and personal situations.

### Reflections

- Spend one day looking at your life through the lens of agreement.
- Look at all of the relationships you have and notice the implicit and explicit agreements that guide your actions.

- Think about the areas in which greater clarity would add to your personal peace and contribute to desired results.

- Choose two or three situations, and, using the models in this book, craft new agreements.

- Reflect on the process, and note any changes in the productivity or satisfaction of the relationships.

# PART V

# When You Need Professional Help

*Part V shows how the model for conflict resolution relates to other methods of resolving conflict and shows what to look for if you need professional help. It explains the value of the legal system and details the role model of the resolutionary.*

# 24

## Using the Power of the Legal System

> It is to law alone that men owe justice and liberty. It is this sal-
> utary organ of the will of all which establishes, in civil right,
> the natural equality between men.
>
> *Jean-Jacques Rousseau*

This book provides a model you can use to resolve conflict and
avoid the high cost of professionals. Unfortunately, everyone
does not aspire to the resolutionary standards advocated here.
Fortunately, we have a system in place for people unwilling
to engage in a peaceful process of resolution: the civil court
system. The system has the teeth to make sure people honor
its decisions. It enforces by coercive power. Our legal system
provides a foundation, leverage, and a place of last resort. The
legal system tells people what their new agreement is.

Because it protects against exploitation, the civil court system and its powers of enforcement hold the heart of liberty. As

discussed in earlier chapters, the system is far from perfect and is subject to abuses in its application, but it surely does protect human rights. The subject of this chapter is how our legal system complements the model for conflict resolution.

## Available Options—Choices on the Continuum

The many dispute resolution services—including those that are part of the legal system—form a continuum. It is important for all consumers of these services to understand where their options are on the continuum. Although "professionals" might blanch at my simplicity, I'll summarize these options from the least to the most invasive:

- *Talking.* It doesn't have a fancy name, but it often works simply and elegantly, as demonstrated in the model for resolving conflict.

- *Creative Design.* The least invasive and most empowering, creative design takes place when two or more parties sit side by side, looking at their joint problem with a mind-set of "how can we best resolve this situation."

- *Negotiation.* Negotiation is a bit more formal, but in some ways it is not different from talking. We negotiate all day, in many different situations. But, in our culture, negotiation has acquired an adversarial component. People have come to approach negotiation with the idea of "winning."

- *Mediation.* When people need some help, they bring in a mediator to facilitate their conversations. The agreement is voluntary; the mediator does not make decisions!

- *Resolution.* Although similar to mediation in that agreements are voluntary, resolution differs because the resolutionary takes more responsibility for getting to resolution. The resolutionary is committed to more than the process; the resolutionary is committed to a resolution that allows people to get on with their lives. The expanded definition of resolution that is found at the beginning of Chapter 21 guides the actions of a resolutionary. Getting to resolution might incorporate any of the options within the continuum.

- *Neutral Evaluation.* In neutral evaluation an expert evaluates the situation and makes an advisory recommendation.

- *Mini-trial.* A mini-trial is similar to neutral evaluation. A mock jury makes an advisory decision that you look to for guidance.

- *Arbitration.* Arbitration is an adversarial proceeding in which the law provides the standards for how issues are decided. It's like a trial, except more informal than civil court proceedings. It can be binding or only advisory.

- *Trials.* Trials are a formal adversary court proceeding—a "civilized" mode of war. Formal rules of evidence determine what the decider takes into consideration.

Remember, you have the power to design a process, and you can creatively combine options to provide the best process for your situation. This was expressed very clearly by Dean Karl Llewellen of the Columbia Law School in the 1930 classic *The Bramble Bush*, a primer for incoming law students:

This doing of something about disputes, this doing of it reasonably, is the business of law. And the people who have the doing in charge, whether they be judges or sheriffs or clerks or jailers or lawyers, are officials of the law. What these officials do about disputes is, to my mind, the law itself.[41]

What the people involved decide, based on the standards they think are important, governs the situation. How a particular situation is resolved is the law for that particular situation!

## Advocacy and Adversarial: Knowing the Difference

Having looked at the broader perspective, let's look at some concerns about today's reality. I remember my introduction to the adversary system. When you probe, listen to the underlying concerns of the other side, and creatively look for solutions that satisfy them and you, accommodation and satisfaction for everyone is possible. Solutions can be invented to accommodate the interests of both sides. Sometimes, strong partisan advocating for each side is the best way to understand all of the parameters of a situation. You must, however, *know the important difference between advocating strongly and being adversarial.* Many people ignore the difference. Advocating is praising the substantive merits of a position that is the result you desire, while being adversarial is as much about demeaning the other position.

You can advocate a position when you know that the other parties are honorable, although they are championing a different position. It is essential to realize that effective resolution comes from relationships created by an honorable attitude. Unfortunately, over the past few years, Rambo tactics have become commonplace. Things were becoming so undisciplined that a Chicago judge issued a report about incivility with recommendations that included rules to guide attorneys' conduct. The prescribed conduct under the new rules reads like manners you forgot to learn from your parents. For me, the unfortunate consequence of unbridled adversarial behavior is that I am moved to advocate getting rid of the adversarial system because it has become so unwieldy. I say this is unfortunate because I believe the existing system can be very effective. The problem is that wholesale gaming of the system has become accepted as standard practice. For me that is sad.

When you choose an advocate, be mindful of the distinction between advocacy and adversarial, the costs listed in Chapter 2, and the suggestions for selecting a professional in Chapter 25. Make sure you choose an effective advocate, someone creative enough to design the best process for your situation. The best thing to do when you encounter an adversarial advocate is choose not to engage. People think it takes only one person to create a fight; in fact, it requires two willing participants. Conversely, it only takes one person to end a fight. If you say "I will not fight," there is no fight. We have much more control than we think!

## Sometimes the Courthouse

In certain situations, formal legal procedure and adjudication is the only way to resolution. You must know when that is the best alternative. Some indications are:

1. When one or more parties will not voluntarily engage in constructive efforts to resolve the matter; for example, a partner takes control of the books of a business, an insurance carrier refuses to make payment, or one party in a divorce refuses to make any kind of payment unless ordered by the court.

2. When one party wants to set a precedent for the future; for example, a manufacturer that is being sued for punitive damages may want to clear its name to prevent future extortion.

3. When public officials can only take action based on judicial authority; this can happen because of uncertainty

that needs legal interpretation, legislative requirement, or the political expediency of shifting responsibility.

4. When you have legal rights you want to enforce.

## Some Thoughts About Our Current System

The existence of the formal legal system, always present in the background, is part of what enables the process of resolution to work. This became clear to me a few years ago when I was talking to a colleague who had taken on the task of bringing conflict resolution skills to the former Soviet Union. His task was formidable. For many years citizens had lived in the paradigm that there was no such thing as conflict. People had little experience with engaging in dialogue to achieve resolution; they were accustomed to receiving answers from an absolute authority.

Even though I personally don't like conflict and do recognize that litigation is a form of war, I know we need a place that will provide fairness for anyone abused—by government, a business, or another individual. Our current safeguards and system of justice provide that place. Given the increasingly complex transactional milieu we inhabit it is time to reexamine them. The foundational principles of the system were designed hundreds of years ago. It is time to revisit some of their corollary premises. Even though the system functions, it is subject to the abuses that arise from the people who play major roles—lawyers, litigants, judges, and juries.

We need a system that helps makes democracy work! Otherwise, we will have the "chaos" of anarchy or the "chaos" of absolute control. The fail-safe of our system provides a remedy against abuse every day—irresponsible manufacturers, abusive governmental action, and irresponsible individuals. But it is time to see if we can do better. I trust this book provides some suggestions for new operational principles.

## Summary

- What separates us from a state of anarchy are the safeguards of a legal system that people can access when they have been abused.

- Before resorting to that system, there is available a continuum of less-invasive processes that work because of the legal system in the background.

## Reflections

- Think about some of the conflicts you are currently facing.

- Given the choices mentioned in this chapter, what do you think the best options are? Why?

# 25

## Choosing a Professional: The Resolutionary

One cool judgment is worth a thousand hasty counsels.

*Woodrow Wilson*

The person you choose as your guide is critical to the kind of resolution you will get. Whether you're alienated from your partner of 15 years, fighting an antitrust battle with the Justice Department, or dissolving a two-year marriage, the style of your advisor is critical.

If you choose a professional to resolve a conflict, make sure you create a partnership and clearly define your desired outcome. Use the agreement process in Chapter 20 to build a joint vision! The process will serve you well. It will help you to choose the right person.

As I mentioned in Chapter 1, contextual research for this book consisted of interviewing about a hundred senior conflict resolution professionals whom I call resolutionaries. Who are

these resolutionaries? They are professionals who know that
their brand of resolution creates lifetime clients. I am fascinated with the way resolutionaries discern real concerns. They
know how to honor and respect what is presented, and how to
find a vessel that holds everyone's concerns.

Their tradition accommodates and balances competing
concerns. Black or white, right or wrong, win or lose is not
the point of their inquiry. They understand effective resolution. Their core message: Fighting is a waste of precious resources—energy, time, money, emotions, and property. They
understand that after every war, the political settlement has to
address the issues. Escalating conflict avoids addressing what
really needs attention.

In this chapter I want to share with you more fully what
resolutionaries do and how to recognize them, so you can select them in an informed way and know what kind of relationship you should expect to have with them.

## What Resolutionaries Do

Resolution is the healing of conflict. The process of resolution
provides a safe environment in which healing can take place.
When disagreement is present, a resolutionary engages in the
following kind of analysis:

1. Who has what concerns in the situation? What is each
   party's reality about the situation?

2. How quickly must action be taken? What is the
   measurable loss and continuing risk of nonresolution?

3. Who is needed for effective resolution?

4. How do we get everyone to the table in the right mood?
   Who needs attitude adjustment, and what's the best way
   to do it?

5. What constraints exist?

6. Are there any laws, regulations, principles, customs, agreements, or other standards for the situation?

7. What future relationships are essential?

8. Are there other special concerns?

9. What is the best action plan? Who will do what, when?

In selecting a resolutionary, I suggest observing the candidate's analytical approach and applying the list above.

## Competencies of a Resolutionary

The following list explains the competencies of a resolutionary. Please use it as criteria for selecting a professional or for evaluating one you have already chosen.

*Collaborative:* A resolutionary enjoys the engagement of working with you toward resolution. Resolutionaries treat you respectfully, are authentic, and learn well with others.

*Common sense:* A resolutionary makes the complex seem simple.

*Confident:* Resolutionaries are clear about the value they contribute. They are not afraid to act on their assessments.

*Creative and innovative:* Resolutionaries invent what they have to do to get the job done.

*Empathy:* Resolutionaries feel for you and your situation, and they honor and legitimize your concerns.

*Fairness/not winning:* Resolutionaries understand that tomorrow is another day and that each day is a victory when you are treated fairly.

*Faith and trust:* The resolutionary knows that every situation can be resolved no matter how bleak it may look—that faith resolves many impossible situations.

*Generating openness:* In resolving conflict, it is essential to have the disagreement in the open. Resolutionaries provide the presence that lets you open up and talk about what happened and your emotions. They create an environment of trust that opens the door to resolution.

*Getting to the core:* Resolutionaries have the uncanny ability to see through to the core of the conflict. They know what must happen to get to the bottom.

*Honesty and integrity:* Trust is at the core of a resolutionary, and you trust resolutionaries because you believe they will effectively advocate your concerns and the concerns of everyone else.

*Intelligence:* Resolutionaries are very smart. They "know" what's happening.

*Judgment:* Resolutionaries have been down the road many times. They know the territory. They have a sixth sense about what will work and what won't.

*Life experience:* Resolutionaries are often bald, or gray, or possess an old soul. They have mileage on them.

*Listening skills:* Resolutionaries understand what is being said, know what's behind the words, and know what's not being said. They know each person must be heard, and they know how to do it. They listen with their eyes and with their entire body.

*Maintaining control of the process:* Resolutionaries watch the process mindfully because, once the process gets out of hand, there is no hope of an efficient resolution.

*Open-minded:* Resolutionaries don't have a vested interest in a particular resolution. They keep the ball in play and let the resolution discover itself.

*Practicality:* Resolutionaries are practical. They do not let personalities or principles stand in the way of sound decisions. They understand what forums are best for working out different kinds of issues.

*Taking care of people:* Resolutionaries know that at the core of all disagreements there is a people-related issue that must be resolved. When you take care of the human concern, the "problem" often takes care of itself.

*Tolerance for conflict:* Resolutionaries remain fair and centered even though the situation is highly charged.

The remainder of the chapter will discuss key aspects you should expect in your relationship with a resolutionary.

## No Hourly Billing

The key to success and the path to partnership in most law firms is your annual number of billable hours. Do you think that impacts professionalism? Resolutionaries know that there is an inherent conflict of interest in hourly billing—resolving the conflict as efficiently as possible versus the self-interest of the attorney, either to make partner or to earn more. One wise advisor I know charges a fixed fee, or he tells clients that he does not know what the cost will be but promises that they will not be unhappy about the fee—and they never are. My suggestion: Agree on a fixed fee.

For intrapersonal conflict, we turn to therapists. They also charge by the hour, and that process of resolution can turn into a lengthy, expensive process. Unfortunately, no one provides firm promises about outcomes.

## Supporting Clients

Resolutionaries support clients in taking personal responsibility. They know that only involved individuals can go to the core of the breakdown in relationships. When you abdicate responsibility, it is difficult to identify and resolve the conflict. This is where most lawyers get sidetracked as they shift the focus to the "legal" issues. By focusing on legal principles and legal issues, effective resolution becomes impossible; the areas that require you to be the most engaged and vulnerable are not addressed.

The core competence of resolutionaries is their ability to lead you to a new vision that returns you to the real business of your life. They support clients' personal growth by keeping the focus on the most vulnerable concerns and talking about them intelligently. Resolutionaries operate from the principle that their job is to lead you to resume collaboration with more effectiveness. Their responsibility is providing the lubrication that gets you back to productivity.

When you develop the habit of more effective communication and collaboration during the resolution process, the pathway you built for the resolution will continue to serve you in the future. This reflects what Professor Robert Baruch Bush calls the transformative aspect of conflict resolution.[42] Building these pathways makes the "legal" issues easy to resolve.

Resolutionaries have a higher calling—upholding the principles embodied in the Ten Commandments. They know these are the laws on which civilized society rests. (Attorneys are part of that tradition, though many young lawyers have little contact with it.) Resolutionaries can rekindle that connection.

*Su wen* describes a single-needle acupuncture treatment so masterful that it catalyzes a sequence of events that cures the difficulty and returns the system to functional harmony and equilibrium. Resolutionaries often provide these elegant outcomes. Their master-strokes are often *su wen* in character. The solutions of the resolutionary reestablish the working relationships that are essential for business, family, or governmental activity. They provide options that contribute to the present and future quality of your life.

## Partnering in Producing Resolution

Clients often do not know what their trusted advisors do for them. Resolutionaries make sure you know what they do before they do it, and why it must be done. They form partnerships with you for producing results. You don't go there to be "fixed." The resolutionary seeks to preserve your resources by letting you do as much as possible. They are also committed to ongoing effectiveness, so they do their best to teach you how to keep the situation on track. When I resolve a situation involving an ongoing relationship, I like to remove myself from the mix and empower the principals to keep the situation resolved.

Consequently, resolutionaries often serve as process designers. The process chosen is essential in determining the outcome. For example, if you have stomach pains and consult a surgeon, you may end up with surgery. A nutritionist, internist, or massage practitioner would have provided a different intervention. Resolutionaries are not locked into a single path or perspective.

## Trust

The importance of trust cannot be overstated. The integrity of the resolutionary is the catalyst that brings the situation to a head. Because of the high level of trust, agreement can result from the resolutionary's sharing an advisory opinion about what he or she thinks is a fair resolution. I have seen these recommendations resolve multi-billion-dollar claims.

Years ago, to support his application to practice law before the courts of another state, my friend Al needed the recommendation of a judge before whom he regularly appeared. He was pleasantly surprised when he read the recommendation. It said that, in contrast to most of the lawyers who appeared before him, the judge was always impressed with Al's candor. He could always be counted on to tell the truth. Al was surprised that others would act any differently.

Expect this level of trust from a resolutionary!

## Creativity

Resolutionaries use their creativity to get the job done. They do whatever it takes. They are not limited by what they think is right or wrong. They often think outside the box. I know a resolutionary who serves as a coach for people who are going into court without counsel. Another resolutionary acts as a consultant, with only the client knowing who is behind the scenes. Whatever role they play, it is always purposeful and chosen consciously.

Resolution does not face some of the formal constraints of traditional processes. It is an arena that has no boundaries. Nor is it for the fainthearted. To make this point, my colleague Jeffrey Kichaven wrote one of my all-time favorite articles: "Mediation Is Not for Sissies."[43] I agree. When there is no "right" way, and you start exploring the emotional relationship issues, you don't know where the process will lead. You must trust your creativity to design the next appropriate step.

## Serving the Situation

Resolutionaries know that the key to what they do lies in serving the needs of the situation. In one situation, a resolutionary was placed on the horns of a dilemma. He was entrusted with the custody of a document that contained essential information about an ongoing dispute in which his primary client was involved. This client was responsible for half of the resolutionary's income.

His client assumed that the resolutionary would turn over the information to him because of their relationship and because no one else would know. The resolutionary refused. His client told him that he would be taking his business elsewhere if the disclosure was not made. The resolutionary still refused. That night he hardly slept, tossing and turning all night. He had one young child and was expecting another; the loss of this client would put his family in immediate financial jeopardy. In the midst of his turmoil, just after he became absolutely certain that his honor was more important than anything, the phone rang. It was his client, calling to apologize for the unethical demand.

The resolutionary thanked his client and shared his concerns: if he disclosed the information, he would lose both his honor and his client. Once it was demonstrated that he was not totally honorable, how could his client trust that the resolutionary would not sell him out? The matter was resolved to everyone's satisfaction the next day, and he gained a client for life.

## A Resolutionary Is Not About Being Nice

**Bryan and Gene.** Bryan, my client, was terminating a long-term relationship with Gene, his business partner. The situation had a number of financial, contractual, personal, and emotional facets. On his lawyer's advice, Gene would not communicate with Bryan. A meeting was arranged. Because Gene was being obstinate, the situation was tense. Bryan thought Gene had no intention of resolving the difficulties between them.

Gene and his attorney mirrored the mood of unreasonableness. It was as though the attorney had some unfinished business to work out with the world, and Bryan's number had come up.

I had a sense of a potential resolution before any conversation with Gene, his partner, or his partner's attorney. The meeting was arranged to resolve the various issues, but many concerns needed addressing. Would a relationship continue? Would it take a new form? If a major contract was secured or if the company was sold to an investor, what would Bryan get? Everyone wanted to explore the old deal and also look at several speculative new ideas.

At the outset I announced, "We are here to resolve this today!" I was crisp, clear, and firm in setting the mood while checking to see if there was hope that resolution was possible, given the animosity. Faced with unreasonableness and personal insults as the meeting unfolded, I became agitated and started pacing. I had to restate the intent of the meeting. I wanted to make sure that it was absolutely clear to everyone: I was there to resolve the matter *that day.* Bryan, who saw no possibility of an early resolution, was getting uncomfortable because of all the hostility. The attacks continued. The room heated up.

As the boiling point neared, my focus sharpened. The hotter the room became, the more settled, calm, cool, purposeful, and agile I became. Speaking firmly and deliberately, I kept my voice icy and fierce: "If you make one more nasty comment, say one more cruel word toward this man, you will regret it. Stop it! Now!"

Bryan had never seen me look or sound like the man who was now his advocate. I was laser-like, clear as crystal, assertive as a radar lock, dangerous, almost lethal. But not out of control, not abusive, not unkind, not uncompassionate. Every cell in my body was aligned. They were all pointing down this attorney's throat. He got the message! Suddenly, he was mute, inanimate, and Gene took over the negotiation.

The mood instantly shifted. In the quiet you could feel the resolution begin to speak its voice. Even in the silence, you could feel the resolution in your chest, coming to the surface. Reaching agreement became a simple matter. The mood and intention that I set helped make that possible.

To do this work effectively, resolutionaries must hold a safe space that allows others to be OK, no matter what is on their mind. They must have the patience to allow each side to say what needs to be said, from whatever the source. I warn my clients about this so they don't feel alone in the resolution process. But *I* am accountable for holding the intention of resolution, and that requires holding a context that is large enough to encompass all parts of the situation.

The knowledge of that necessity informs every instinct of my being. Whatever must be done, will be done. Don't make the mistake of thinking that the way of the heart is always nice and sweet or that elegant conflict resolution is always pretty. A resolutionary can be lethal. Sometimes you have no choice.

People from all over the country often ask where they can find a resolutionary. I have trained a number of people and expect to expand that training as I roll out a new e-learning program. Beyond that, it is critical to stay mindful as you select someone. Stay mindful as you evaluate them against the competencies suggested above. As you narrow your search ask for references you can call or email and ask those references how well they were taken care of, how involved they were in the process, and what the resolved relationships are like today. Here's a resource you can use to make your evaluation.

## Evaluating a Potential Resolutionary

As you select a professional, ask yourself (trust your gut) if the person you want to work with has the following characteristics:

| | | |
|---|---|---|
| Collaborative | Common sense | Confident |
| Creative and innovative | Empathy | Fairness/not winning |
| Faith and trust | Generating openness | Getting to the core |
| Honesty and integrity | Intelligence | Judgment |
| Life experience | Listening skills | Open-minded |
| Practicality | Serve the situation | Taking care of people |
| Tolerance for conflict | Trust | No hourly billing |
| Supporting client's resolution | Partner | Maintaining control of the process |

I suggest that, unless you believe they have at least 20 of the 24 characteristics listed above, look for someone else.

### *Summary*

- In choosing someone to help you resolve a conflict when you have already tried, make sure you select a person who will partner with you, not someone who will do it for you.

- Look for someone who listens, has independent opinions, will set a fixed fee, talks about the human aspect of the situation, and doesn't take him or herself too seriously.

- The role model of the resolutionary provides a standard to be followed.

### Reflections

- What qualities are most important for the professional who helps you?
- Take the time to write them down.
- Do you know anyone who fits the bill? Describe them.
- For 21 days—the time it takes to "install" a new habit—act like you are a resolutionary.

Life is too short to be little.

*Disraeli*

# Part VI

## The Power of Resolution

*Now that you understand how the conflict resolution model works, Part VI projects what your life will be like when you adopt and master the principles and practices of resolution.*

# 26

# Building a Culture of Agreement and Resolution

We look forward to the time when the Power of Love will replace the Love of Power. Then will our world know the blessings of Peace.

*Gladstone*

We can become the change we are waiting for!

Often the aggregation of simple actions by many can have a huge impact. This is reflected by a variety of recent innovations: micro loans in India, local agricultural policies sponsored by the World Bank, the Cultural Revolution in China, the Women's movement, Lady Bird Johnson's highway clean-up, and the Green movement. All represent small individual actions that together constituted a movement that had a profound large-scale impact.

If we change our kids' education, act civilly toward each other in our families and communities, and adopt new business practices, we can become the change we are waiting for. By taking these small actions, large results would follow.

It all starts with you! and me! and your neighbor! and your significant other! and your family! and your colleagues! and your boss! and your mayor! and your city council people! and your state representatives! and your congressperson!.... and your ...!

This chapter represents how ordinary lives could be very different if individuals adopted new behaviors. As you read the chapter, imagine how your life would be different if more people used resolutionary skills.

## Tuesday

It's Tuesday morning. You had a fitful night. Just before you fell asleep, Matthew, your husband of nine years, broke the news that his company finally offered him the job he has been pining for—implementing a new companywide employee development program. He had accepted on the spot, even though the position requires immediate relocation from San Francisco to Cleveland. You politely offered congratulations, but your reaction is mixed. You are happy for him, but you don't know how you can support the move, given the impact on your career and on your 14- and 15-year-old daughters from a prior marriage. You are also angry because he did not consult with you before making the decision.

The situation is complicated further because you have just been made partner in your group medical practice and you promised your kids that they can finish high school in San Francisco. At the moment you don't know what to do. Keeping to yourself, you quietly dress and head off to your office.

At the office you find that you have just been put in charge of the support team of nurses and staff. Your office manager recently attended a workshop on self-directed work teams, and he wants to implement that concept in the practice. You have to work with him because you are on both the management and finance committees. Recently, staff members have been complaining because they want more control over their work. Forget the notion that you get to give orders because you're the boss. Those days are gone!

Around noon, the HMO that accounts for 35% of your business calls to say it is signing an agreement with a local hospital that may result in your losing all or a portion of the business. You just want to go back to bed! There are two phone messages waiting when you return from lunch. One from your mother, and one from the secretary of the Board of Education, of which you are the president. Your mother is upset because your father is insisting on moving to Arizona, and your board is being threatened by a teachers' strike. Mercury must have gone retrograde! You wonder what the afternoon will bring.

You have your hands full, but you calmly observe the strong emotional reactions you have to all of these potential disasters. You have faith that you will get through these crises with little fuss. You are confident that all of these conflicts will have great outcomes for everyone concerned. You remind yourself that an attitude of resolution will serve you best. Since you have so much on your plate, it's critical to remain focused and not waste emotional energy.

After some reflection you sit down and make a prioritized list of what needs attention and the action you will take:

1. Call the HMO, find out why it is changing hospitals, and schedule a meeting.

2. Call the Board of Education and schedule an emergency meeting with the president of the teachers' union.

3. Call your mom and dad, tell them you'll see them Saturday for lunch and get their situation resolved then.

4. Call Matthew and tell him you (a) love him and are very proud of him, (b) you want to take him out to dinner on Saturday night, just the two of you, and (c) that you need to speak with him about your concerns over his promotion and how it will impact the family.

5. Call Roberto, your office manager, and schedule a meeting to discuss the idea of reorganizing the support staff.

As you check off the list, you feel proud of your ability to move into a state of resourcefulness. You acknowledge how fortunate you feel to have a roadmap to take you through these situations to a place of resolution.

First, you call the executive director of the HMO and request a meeting for that evening, after you have finished with your last patient. You tell him that his HMO is your most valued client, that you will do what you must to keep its business, and you want to talk about why the HMO is considering another provider. You are pleasantly surprised at how receptive he is to meeting with you. You acknowledge to yourself how valuable the attitude of resolution is.

Then you decide to call the president of the teachers' union yourself. You say you want to meet with her to resolve the outstanding issues in the contract negotiation. You know she is sensitive to the effect of a strike on the community. The teachers must be very concerned about their contract if they are considering a strike, and it is your intention to listen to the concerns and reach an agreement. She acknowledges your contacting her directly, your willingness to move quickly beyond posturing, and the sincerity of your message. You feel you are picking up momentum as you agree to meet Wednesday after work and keep going as long as needed.

You call and find your mother in a state of high drama. The thought of moving away from her children, grandchildren, friends, and the house she has lived in for 40 years is making her crazy. Even more disconcerting, your father won't discuss it. His mind is made up, and that's it. You tell her you will call him and that you promise to get it resolved over lunch on Saturday. She calms down a bit. You call your father and tell him he is being inconsiderate by making such a big decision unilaterally (as your husband did). You ask him to have lunch with you and your mother. You ask him to come to lunch with an open mind. He agrees to apologize for not consulting your mother and to come to lunch and keep an open mind, but he says he is still moving. You say "Thanks, I'll see you Saturday."

You get your husband on the phone. You tell him you love him, and that your relationship will survive whatever career choices need to be made. You tell him that even though you know how important the promotion is to him, you were upset that he didn't discuss it with you. It flies in the face of all the covenants your marriage is based on. You ask him to have dinner with you Saturday night, at his restaurant of choice, so you can fully discuss and quickly resolve the situation. He accepts. You sense he is holding onto his "male career prerogative," so you know the conversation will not be simple. You assure him again that you want to support him and understand how important the position is to him.

You call your office manager and set up a meeting with him for early the next morning.

You take a deep breath and reflect on how good you feel. Even though the situations are challenging, you have taken a proactive posture with all of them. The balls are in play, and even though the discussions won't be easy, they are already moving forward. You feel good as you start your afternoon schedule of patients.

On your way to the HMO, you start thinking about the history of the relationship between your medical practice and the HMO. You can't understand the reasons for its change of heart. You decide that your objective for the meeting is to leave with the basis for a new agreement, and that the most important thing you want to find out is the conditions of satisfaction for a successful ongoing relationship.

You exchange pleasant greetings with Dan Johnson, and then get right to the point. You ask Dan what's going on. He says that the changes have nothing to do with any performance problems on your part, that the situation is a result of a corporate acquisition of their company. Their new parent has an agreement with the parent of the local hospital. He tells you that nothing is written in stone and the primary concern remains the best possible treatment for their patients. You tell him that it is important to you not to lose any of their business and that you will do what is necessary to maintain their business and the relationship. You want to craft an agreement that will make explicit the "partnership" that has been implicit. Most important, you want the information that will enable your organization to be their ideal provider.

He agrees. You proceed to work through all the elements of the agreement template that you have learned. You discuss a vision for patient service, the promises each of you must deliver on to enable that level of service, how you will measure satisfaction, concerns each of you has, and a specific method for resolving conflict. You thank him for his participation and say you will put the understandings in writing for each of you to reference. As you are about to leave, he says "Thank you. I have never felt so thoroughly listened to about what we want from our independent providers. If we can live up to the agreement we have just crafted, we will be functioning within a partnership few believe is possible." You say thank you and remind him that this is only the first step.

That night your husband is especially attentive. He wants to talk about the move and your feelings. You give him a kiss and say that you think it is a good idea to hold off on the discussion until dinner Saturday—that the notion of each of you having some time for reflection will do you both some good.

## Wednesday

First thing the next morning you meet with your office manager, Roberto. He is excited about making the entire office support staff of 22 people a self-directed work team. You ask what that is. Roberto says it is an organizational form in which the team members set goals, performance standards, schedules, compensation, and evaluation criteria. You tell him that to you that means they will run the show in terms of their work.

Given some of your recent managerial reading about increasing productivity, you like the idea. An article you read reported that most workers perform far below their capacity because they have little respect for the people managing them and for how the managers evaluate them. The article's ideas made sense to you. You see self-directed work teams as a step in the right direction. You give the idea your blessings. You also request that Roberto set up the process in which an agreement between the team and the practice is put in place, as well as agreements between each individual and both their team and the practice. Your aim has been to get the full benefit of what each individual can give to the practice. You see the team concept as a great way to implement an open environment—developing each person to be fully responsible for their own tasks. You tell Roberto how pleased you are with the new structure that will be put in place. You make yourself available to support the process in whatever way you can.

The meeting with the president of the teachers' union has you filled with anxiety because of the potential impact of a strike. You ask her if the meeting can be "off the record" because you want to have a frank conversation. You tell her you have recently learned about a process designed to bring every element of the conflict out in the open, and ask if she will participate. She agrees, on the condition that you lead the way. You have already stated your intention to do your best to resolve the situation. You emphasize how essential authenticity is to get the outcome you both desire.

You each tell your respective stories. Then you yourself serve as both guide and participant in a completion process. What is quickly uncovered is that, on the prior advice of counsel, each of you has been posturing and withholding critical information. Their advice, though sound within the traditional legal paradigm, has promoted a game of brinksmanship. The conversations let you step into the shoes of the union president. Now that you have a complete picture of the situation, you see a potential resolution. You propose a solution. She accepts. An agreement in principle is reached, to be implemented by your attorneys. Given your success, you ask if she wants to meet next week to work on an "agreement for results" that could create real partnership between the teachers and the administration.

You feel fulfilled as you pull into your driveway. After the completion process with the teachers' union president, you turned into collaborators looking for the solution that would take care of everyone's concerns. The requests of the teachers were seen as legitimate, as were yours. You became creative designers, looking together at the big picture you both had a stake in resolving. Tomorrow is another day, but so far you are three for three!

## Thursday and Friday

You move through the rest of the week with a sense of elation. You are beginning to trust the notion that conflicts provide an opportunity for the highest expression of yourself. Being conflict-averse, as most of us are, you never realized that working through to resolution could enhance and affirm your life so much. You are so pleased you made the choice to learn a systematic way to get to the other side.

When you hit the pillow on Friday, you have a better sense of who you are. You sleep soundly, once again resisting your husband's attempt to talk about his promotion.

## Saturday

After your morning hospital rounds, you arrive for the pow-wow with Mom and Dad. It amazes you that after 40 years of marriage your parents don't have a clue about how to engage in a productive conversation in which real communication takes place. They are still living in a world of fault, blame, being right, and withdrawal. One divorce and a number of difficult relationships have forced you to examine the arena of human interaction. You realize that every generation has new horizons to explore.

You ask Mom to tell her story. Then you turn to Dad. You have to sit on both of them to prevent interruptions and editorial comments. You ask them what has worked about the marriage, and they lighten up as they recall a lifetime of wonderful memories. You ask about what doesn't work, and you hear the kind of things that are bound to arise between two human beings who have shared a lifetime. When you ask them to forgive each other, and themselves, they do. When you ask them to thank each other, and God, for bringing them together, they do. When you ask about what else needs to be said, they both

say that they don't care where they live, as long as they are together. They each take responsibility for having been inconsiderate and obstinate.

You can see the resolution forming. You turn to them and
ask if either has a proposal. Dad says he will give up his plans
to move—that it is not worth the guilt and aggravation. Mom
says OK, but she wants him to have as much Arizona as he
needs. They agree to spend a fourth of their time in Arizona
and the rest in San Francisco.

Now you can have a swim and catch up on some paper-
work before dinner with Matthew. As the cooling water runs
over your body, you start to think about your upcoming conversation with your husband. Deep inside, you are nervous and
feeling very vulnerable. You don't really know where this is going. The marriage will change. At worst, it may end. Watching
Mom and Dad in action provided some inspiration in terms
of the value of longevity in a relationship. As you move into a
flip-turn and push hard off the wall, the messages of all your
teachers provide healthy guidance:

1. A key to life is knowing that all we can do in any
   situation is:

   Be present in the moment.

   Listen—externally and internally.

   Speak what is true for you.

   Do not be attached to particular outcomes.

2. The most vulnerable and most important place in the
   continuum towards resolution lies in "not knowing"
   the answer. Our ability to stay in that place until clarity
   arrives is the key to uncovering the best outcome.

3. The best framework for any difficult situation is to "learn"
   our way through it.

Now you feel prepared! You return home and dress for dinner. You and Matthew head to his favorite restaurant. Despite the difficulty of the situation, you feel more beautiful and alive than you have ever felt. You are ready for the conversation.

After ordering, you open the conversation. Since you know the resolution process, you orient him to the structure of the conversation and the attitude of resolution you would like to adopt. You tell him that you will be looking for a creative resolution that will take care of both of you. Because of your clarity and the mood of resolution that you have established, he agrees to participate fully. You take a deep breath and start to tell your "story."

You tell him how much you care for him, how important your marriage is, and how much you value what you have built. You tell him how much respect you have for his achievements and how you don't want to stand in the way of his advancement. You tell him that you want to see everyone in the situation satisfied. You tell him that you can't leave San Francisco, but that you won't stand in his way. You feel lighter as the words pour out of your heart. He tells you about his anguish over the juncture you have reached—his fear and his desire. He feels that he must choose between you and his career, and it is a choice he does not want to make. He knows there is no right or wrong in the situation, that the only way to get to the bottom is to respect each other. He understands your concerns, but it seems clear to him that his whole life, all that he has worked for, is tied up in this moment of destiny.

You both feel suspended in a womb-like cocoon as you continue the birthing process of finding resolution. Your dialogue is like Michelangelo chiseling away at the excess to uncover his masterpiece. As you begin the completion process, your energy starts to flow. You delineate what works in your marriage: the foundation and oasis it provides; the good company; intellectual stimulation; romance; minimal amount of friction; economic partnership; raising the children; respect; autonomy; vacations; love; the fact that it functions when so many marriages are falling apart. There are things that don't work: career demands of time, focus, and energy; Matthew's sometimes acting the way he thinks a man should act, like his acceptance of the position without discussion; your ex-husband's impact on your kids; career orientations of both of you; your fear and vulnerability. This is not as difficult as you thought it would be.

You are in agreement about what you have to be thankful for: that you found each other after both of you had unsuccessful marriages; your home, children, family and friends; your respective careers; the grounding your marriage provides. Identifying who you each have to forgive is instructive for both of you. You forgive Matthew for being overly protective of the girls and for the times he doesn't honor your career needs as he honors his own; his sometimes excessive flirtations; his broken promises around household maintenance; his being overly critical of your cooking. You forgive him for his success and ambition—the drive he has demonstrated has provided a healthy income and put you through medical school, but it has also resulted in the current crossroad. Matthew forgives you for your school-board activities; your refusal to join him on skiing trips; your messy home office; and your cats. Most of all he forgives you for your successful career and the devotion you have to your parents, children, and the community.

As you forgive each other for the positive attributes of your separate lives, a mood of respect and admiration begins to emerge. You see each other in a more profound way. An element of admiration and support for the concerns and aspirations of the other starts to surface. You each experience the grief that change brings. You both feel the sadness of disappointed expectation about what you thought your life would continue to be. You feel some fear about the changes and the day-to-day separation. But the resolution seems clear to both of you.

To be complete, you each needed to say that you were committed to making the transition, the separation, and the marriage work.

It was agreed that Matthew would move to Cleveland, set up housekeeping, and return at least every other weekend. You left all the other details to be worked out later. One thing that was agreed was that you were partners for life; nothing would get in the way of that. The rest of the evening was deeply intimate, a closeness you will never forget. When you reviewed the conversation and your feelings about it, you had a sense of well-being beyond any you ever felt. You knew in the deepest part of yourself that this man was your mate and that you were just taking off on another great adventure together. You started to see all the opportunities present in the new era—the era you named "Separation, Growth, Autonomy, and Adulthood."

## Year End

At the end of the year you reflected on the value of the attitude of resolution, and your growing mastery of the resolution process. You and Matthew are both thriving. The marriage could not be healthier. Although the transition was not simple, instead of often being frustrated and torn by the conflict of other priorities, you seem to be spending more quality time together. Each of you is freer to devote full attention to the vocation and causes you are committed to. And when you come together, it's like a honeymoon.

Matthew is being considered for a division presidency. You have been made a full partner in your practice. The agreement you put in place with the HMO was so well received they are sending you more patients than you have time for—so you added two more physicians to your staff. Your office staff has increased its productivity by 33%, and the mood around the office is one of teamwork and support. Your agreement with the teachers' union was hailed as an innovative model—both the procedure and the substance. You have been appointed to the State Board of Education and have been traveling around the state teaching others how you did it. Your parents' establishment in an Arizona retirement home has added a level of zest to their marriage—they couldn't be healthier or happier.

As you get ready to ring in the new year, you feel grateful for the lack of conflict in your life. You are producing results way beyond expectation—and having a great time. You kiss your napping husband and roll over to let the warmth of the sun caress your face.

# Preparing for a Conflict Resolution Process

In preparation for a conflict that needs resolution, use this worksheet to begin planning what you'll need to address before engaging in the dialogue. Reflect on the questions to help you see what you need. Take the steps to do what you need to be ready.

1. What is it, and briefly what's your "story" about it (how do you talk to yourself about the conflict)? What is really at stake for you? For them?

2. On a scale of 1–5 (1 being slightly agitated, 5 being gripped by emotion), how do you feel about the other people involved and engaging in the dialogue. Are you ready to engage in effective collaborative negotiation? What will enable you to do that?

3. Can you treat the resolution process as an opportunity to listen and learn?

4. Can you participate with practicality, and with open mind and open heart, and let go of any need for revenge?

5. Can you accept that with trust, good faith, and creativity everyone can win and get what they need?

6. What aspects of the resolution process are you unsure of?

7. Do you need a third-party facilitator? Why?

8. Are you willing to have compassion and stand in the shoes of others involved?

9. Are you fully aware of what the conflict is and what it could cost you? Are you ready to let go, forgive, and make an agreement for the future?

10. What other support will empower you to engage authentically?

# Cycle of Resolution Facilitation Tutorial

### *Step 1. Your Attitude of Resolution*

Let people know: You are there to facilitate, not to decide or referee; steps 1–4 are for clearing the air, setting the table; the process is about creating a shared vision for the future; you may hear things you do not like (no need to respond, they are the perceptions of another, not "the truth"); ground rules include no cross talk—this is not about debating, winning or finding truth; listening is critical; one person speaks at a time.

### *Step 2. Stories: Telling and Listening*

Ask people to tell the story they have about the situation.

Tell them they cannot do this wrong.

Remind everyone to listen to their own story.

Let people know they will have ample opportunity to respond and that it is important not to interrupt while others are telling their story.

### *Step 3. Listening for a Vision of Resolution*

Tell each person to listen for real interests and concerns and think about a solution that addresses everyone's interests.

### *Step 4. Getting Current and Complete*

Explain that you will ask a series of questions and that responses will be "popcorn" style; whoever has something to say will say it.

Ask the questions . . .

*For longer-term, more familiar relationships:*

1. What worked about the relationship, partnership, or venture?

2. What didn't work?

3. Who do you need to forgive and for what?

4. Who do you need to apologize to and for what?

5. Who do you need to thank and for what?

6. What else do you need to say so that you are complete enough to say "Today is a good day to die"?

7. Do you have any requests?

8. Declare that the conflict is current in the moment and complete! You must say it!

9. What's the new era? The new era is _____.

*For business and professional relationships:*

1. What was effective about the original agreement? What worked?

2. What was ineffective? What didn't work?

3. What about your own behavior are you sorry for? (apology)

4. What can you say by way of compassion for the other participants' shortcomings or incompetence? (forgiveness)

5. What can you say by way of respect for the other people, their competence, their contribution, and their conduct in the situation? (thanks)

6. Pretending for a moment that you will never have another opportunity to speak about this matter, what else do you want to say?

7. Do you have any requests?

8. Declare completion!

9. What's the new era?

### *Step 5. Reaching Agreement in Principle*

Get people to agree on what the future will look like. Suggest that it is now time to communicate and negotiate with each other.

### *Step 6. Crafting the New Agreement*

Facilitate creation of a new shared vision using the elements of agreement:

1. Intent and vision

2. Roles

3. Promises

4. Time/value

5. Measurements of satisfaction

6. Concerns and fears

7. Renegotiation

8. Consequences

9. Conflict resolution

10. Agreement?

### *Step 7. Resolution*

Acknowledge and thank people for their hard work and perseverance.

Let people know that the hard work begins now because they will be stepping out of the container you have been holding and it is common for people to forget the work they have done and slip back into holding the other as enemy.

Tell people it will be critical to be vigilant about their intention and capacity to be an emotionally intelligent conscious communicator.

# Local Actions You Can Take

- Engage and teach your neighbors.
- Form learning and study groups.
- Organize youth events and competitions.
- Request that local boards of education introduce programs.
- Request your public library sponsor a book focused program.
- Declare your town a Collaboration Community.
- Encourage mediation in resolving local conflicts.
- Develop a community mediation program.
- Encourage local media to take a less adversarial attitude.
- Celebrate/publicize success of local non-adversarial resolutions.
- Support the proposal creating a cabinet-level U.S. Department of Peace

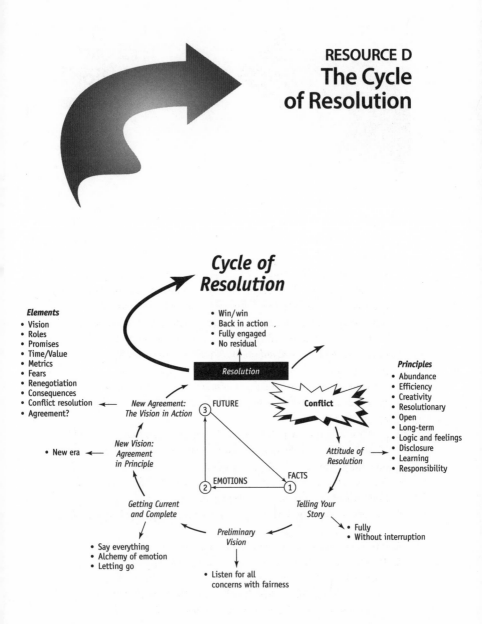

# The Cycle of Resolution

## Cycle of Resolution

**Elements**
- Vision
- Roles
- Promises
- Time/Value
- Metrics
- Fears
- Renegotiation
- Consequences
- Conflict resolution
- Agreement?

- Win/win
- Back in action
- Fully engaged
- No residual

**Resolution**

**Principles**
- Abundance
- Efficiency
- Creativity
- Resolutionary
- Open
- Long-term
- Logic and feelings
- Disclosure
- Learning
- Responsibility

**New Agreement:**
*The Vision in Action*

FUTURE ③

**Conflict**

*New Vision:*
*Agreement*
*in Principle*

- New era

② EMOTIONS

FACTS ①

*Attitude of*
*Resolution*

*Getting Current*
*and Complete*

- Say everything
- Alchemy of emotion
- Letting go

*Preliminary*
*Vision*

*Telling Your*
*Story*

- Fully
- Without interruption

- Listen for all
  concerns with fairness

# Notes

1. Collaboration is a key driver of overall performance of companies around the world. Its impact is twice as significant as a company's aggressiveness in pursuing new market opportunities (strategic orientation) and five times as significant as the external market environment (market turbulence). Collaboration can positively impact each of the gold standards of performance—profitability, profit growth, and sales growth—to determine a company's overall performance in the marketplace. *Impact of Collaboration on Business Performance*, Frost & Sullivan (2007), sponsored by Verizon and Microsoft.
2. See "The Psychology of Mediation: Issues of Self and Identity" and "The IDR Cycle" by Elizabeth Bader at http://elizabethbader.com/pdf_publications/SelfandIdentity.pdf.
3. A client who had a flair for promotion coined this phrase as I guided him through a series of sensitive negotiations.
4. National Center for State Courts, www.ncsconline.org; Federal Judicial Center, www.fjc.gov.
5. Interview with Alvin Toffler, *Wired* magazine, November 1993.
6. The story about BQ is found in Joel Barker, *Paradigms: The Business of Discovering the Future* (New York, Harper Business, 1993).
7. Jerry B. Harvey, *The Abilene Paradox and Other Meditations on Management* (New York, Lexington Books, 1988).

8. Steven R. Covey, *Seven Habits of Highly Effective People* (New York, Simon & Schuster, 1989).

9. Roger Dawson, *Secrets of Power Negotiating* (Hawthorne, NJ, Career Press, 1995).

10. Bruce Tuckman, Developmental sequence in small groups. *Psychological Bulletin* 63, 1965, pp. 384–99.

11. In Daniel Goleman's thesis, self-awareness is the foundation of emotional intelligence. Daniel Goleman, *Emotional Intelligence* (New York, Bantam, 1995.)

12. See Bader, note 2.

13. Angelis Arrien, *The Four Fold Way* (New York, HarperCollins, 1993).

14. The Magazine of the Writer's Guild of America (2003), 7(2), p. 48.

15. John Kabat-Zinn, *Wherever You Go, There You Are* (New York, Hyperion, 1994).

16. Margaret Wheatley, *Leadership and the New Science* (San Francisco, Berrett-Koehler, 1992).

17. Ken Wilbur, *History of Everything* (Boston, Shambhala, 2001); Eckart Tolle, *The Power of Now* (Novato, CA, New World Library, 1999) ; also see Verna Allee's work about value networks at www.vernaallee. com.

18. Robert Benjamin, The mediator as trickster, *Family Mediation Quarterly* 13 (San Francisco, Jossey-Bass, Fall 1995).

19. Leonard L. Riskin, The contemplative lawyer: On the potential contributions of mindfulness meditation to law students and lawyers and their clients, *Harvard Negotiation Law Review* 7:1–66 (June 2002), the centerpiece of a symposium on mindfulness in law and ADR). A webcast of the live symposium held at Harvard Law School in March 2002 is available at http://www.pon.harvard.edu/events/mindfulness-in-the-law-adr/.

20. Edward DeBono, *Conflicts, A Better Way to Resolve Them* (London, Harrap Limited, 1985).

21. The term *open book management* appears in Jack Stack, *The Great Game of Business* (New York, Doubleday, 1992).

22. Don Tapscott and Anthony Williams, *Wikinomics* (New York, Penguin, 2006).

23. A recent development in the construction industry is the concept of "partnering," in which all parties to major projects attend a meeting before construction begins. At the meeting they agree on how they will work together and how they will resolve conflict. For more information see www.orgmetrics.com and www.partneringinstitute. org.

24. Michelle and Dennis Reina, *Trust and Betrayal in the Workplace* (San Francisco, Berrett-Koehler, 1998, 2007); Steven M.R. Covey, *The Speed of Trust* (New York, Simon & Schuster, 2008).
25. See Goleman, note 10.
26. Rachel Naomi Remen, MD, *Kitchen Table Wisdom* (New York, Riverhead Books, 1996).
27. Mehrabian, Albert, and Ferris, Susan R. "Inference of Attitudes from Nonverbal Communication in Two Channels," *Journal of Consulting Psychology* 31(3), June 1967, pp. 248–58.
28. Scott Peck, MD, *The Road Less Traveled* (New York, Simon & Schuster, 1978).
29. Bill Lamond, a trainer and consultant, first introduced me to a form of "The Completion Process."
30. Robert M. Bramson, *Coping with Difficult People* (New York, Anchor-Doubleday, 1981).
31. Max DePree, *Leadership Is an Art* (New York, Doubleday, 1989).
32. Deepak Chopra, MD, *Creating Affluence* (San Rafael, CA, New World Library, 1993).
33. Napoleon Hill, *Think and Grow Rich* (New York, Fawcett Crest, [rev. ed.], 1960).
34. Maxwell Maltz, MD, *Psycho-Cybernetics* (New York, Simon & Schuster, 1960).
35. James Kouzes and Barry Posner, *The Leadership Challenge* (San Francisco, Jossey-Bass, 1987).
36. Max DePree, *Leadership Jazz* (New York, Currency Doubleday, 1992).
37. Humberto Maturana, *The Tree of Knowledge* (Boston, Shambhala, 1992).
38. Steven R. Covey, *Principle Centered Leadership* (New York, Summit, 1991).
39. The principle of self-organization is also the premise of Margaret Wheatley and Myron Kellner-Rogers, *A Simpler Way* (San Francisco, Berrett-Koehler, 1996).
40. Dr. Fernando Flores called these areas "Domains of Permanent Concern."
41. Karl Llewellen, *The Bramble Bush* (New York, Oceana, 1930).
42. Robert A. Baruch Bush and Joseph P. Folger, *The Promise of Mediation* (San Francisco, Jossey-Bass, 1994).
43. Jeffrey G. Kichaven, Mediation is not for sissies, *Los Angeles County Bar Association Litigation Newsletter* 13(2), Winter 1996.

# Bibliography

Aburdine, Patricia and John Naisbitt. *Megatrends for Women* (New York, Villard, 1992).

Acland, Andrew Floyer. *A Sudden Outbreak of Common Sense* (London, Hutchinson Business, 1990).

Adams, Marilee. *Change Your Questions, Change Your Life* (San Francisco, Berrett-Koehler, 2004).

Arbinger Institute. *The Anatomy of Peace* (San Francisco, Berrett-Koehler, 2006).

Arbinger Institute. *Leadership and Self-Deception* (San Francisco, Berrett-Koehler, 2002).

Arrien, Angelis. *The Four Fold Way* (New York, Harper Collins, 1993).

Avery, Christopher. *Teamwork Is an Individual Skill* (San Francisco, Berrett-Koehler, 2001).

Axelrod, Richard. *Terms of Engagement* (San Francisco, Berrett-Koehler, 2000).

Bandler, Richard. *Using Your Brain—For a Change* (Moab, UT, Real People Press, 1985).

Bandler, Richard and John Grinder. *Frogs into PRINCES* (Moab, UT, Real People Press, 1979).

Barker, Joel. *Paradigms: The Business of Discovering the Future* (New York, HarperBusiness, 1993).

Beyerlein, Michael and Sue Freedman, Craig McGee, and Linda Moran. *Beyond Teams* (San Francisco, Jossey-Bass, 2003).

Block, Peter. *Community* (San Francisco, Berrett-Koehler, 2008).

Block, Peter. *The Answer to How Is Yes* (San Francisco, Berrett-Koehler, 2002).

Bowling, Daniel and David Hoffman (Eds.) *Bringing Peace into the Room* (San Francisco, Jossey-Bass, 2003).

Bramson, Robert M. *Coping with Difficult People* (New York, Anchor-Doubleday, 1981).

Briskin, Alan. *The Stirring of Soul in the Workplace* (San Francisco, Jossey-Bass, 1996).

Bush, Robert A. Baruch and Joseph P. Folger. *The Promise of Mediation* (San Francisco, Jossey-Bass, 1994).

Chaleff, Ira. *The Courageous Follower* (San Francisco, Berrett-Koehler, 1995).

Champy, James. *Reengineering Management* (New York, Harper Business, 1995).

Childre, Doc and Howard Martin. *The Heartmath Solution* (San Francisco, HarperCollins, 1999).

Chopra, Deepak. *Creating Affluence* (San Rafael, CA, New World Library, 1993).

Coelho, Paul. *The Alchemist* (New York, Harper San Francisco, 1993).

Coleman, David and Stewart Levine. *Collaboration 2.0* (San Jose, Happy About, 2008).

Costantino, Cathy A. and Christina Sickles Marchant. *Designing Conflict Management Systems* (San Francisco, Jossey-Bass, 1996).

Covey, Steven R. *Principle Centered Leadership* (New York, Summit, 1991).

Covey, Steven R. *Seven Habits of Highly Effective People* (New York, Simon & Schuster, 1989).

Covey, Stephen M.R. *The Speed of Trust* (New York, Simon & Schuster, 2008).

Crumm, Tom. *The Magic of Conflict* (New York, Simon & Shuster, 1987).

Dana, Daniel. *Talk It Out* (Amherst, MA, Human Resource Development Press, 1989).

Dass, Ram and Paul Gorman. *How Can I Help: Stories and Reflections on Service* (New York, Alfred A. Knopf, 1987).

Davis, Laura. *I Thought We'd Never Speak Again* (New York, Harper-Collins, 2002).

Dawson, Roger. *Secrets of Power Negotiating* (Hawthorne, NJ, Career Press, 1995).

DeBono, Edward. *Conflicts, A Better Way to Resolve Them* (London, Harrap Limited, 1985).

DeBono, Edward. *Serious Creativity* (New York, HarperBusiness, 1992).

DePree, Max. *Leadership Is an Art* (New York, Doubleday, 1989).

DePree, Max. *Leadership Jazz* (New York, Doubleday, 1992).

Dibble, David. *The New Agreements in the Workplace* (New York, Emeritus, 2002).

Dukes, E. Franklin and Marina A. Piscolish, John B. Stephens. *Reaching for Higher Ground in Conflict Resolution* (San Francisco, Jossey-Bass, 2000).

Dyer, Wayne. *Gifts from Eykis* (New York, Simon & Schuster, 1983).

Edelman, Joel. *The Tao of Negotiation* (New York, HarperBusiness, 1993).

Eisler, Riane. *The Chalice and the Blade* (San Francisco, Harper & Row, 1987).

Fisher, Roger and Scott Brown. *Getting Together* (Boston, Houghton Mifflin, 1988).

Fisher, Roger and William Ury. *Getting to Yes* (Boston, Houghton Mifflin, 1981).

Fritz, Robert. *Creating What You Always Wanted To* (Salem, MA, DMA, 1985).

Goldberg, Marilee. *The Art of the Question* (New York, Wiley, 1998).

Goleman, Daniel. *Emotional Intelligence* (New York, Bantam, 1995).

Hanh, Thich Nhat. *Being Peace* (Berkeley, Parallax Press, 1987); *Touching Peace* (Berkeley, Parallax Press, 1992); and *Peace Is Every Step* (New York, Bantam, 1992).

Harvey, Jerry B. *The Abilene Paradox and other Meditations on Management* (New York, Lexington Books, 1988).

Hawkins, David R. *Power vs. Force* (Carlsbad, CA, Hay House, 2002).

Henry, James F. and Jethro K. Lieberman. *The Manager's Guide to Resolving Legal Disputes* (New York, Harper & Row, 1985).

Hill, Napoleon. *Think and Grow Rich* (New York, Fawcett-Crest, 1937 [rev. ed. 1960]).

Holman, Peggy and Tom Devane, Steve Cady. *The Change Handbook* (San Francisco, Berrett-Koehler, 2007).

Howard, Nigel. *Confrontation Analysis* (Vienna, VA, CCRP, 1999).

Jordan-Evans, Sharon and Beverly Kaye. *Love 'Em or Lose 'Em* (San Francisco, Berrett-Koehler, 1999).

Kabat-Zinn, Jon. *Wherever You Go, There You Are* (New York, Hyperion, 1994).

Kaner, Sam with Duane Berger, Sarah Fisk, Lenny Lind, and Catherine Toldi. *Facilitators' Guide to Participatory Decision Making* (Gabriola

Island, BC, New Society, 1996).

Katzenbach, John R. and Douglas K. Smith. *The Wisdom of Teams* (Cambridge, Harvard Business School Press, 1993).

Keen, Sam. *Fire in the Belly: On Being a Man* (New York, Bantam, 1991).

Keeva, Steven. *Transforming Practices* (Chicago, Contemporary, 1999).

Knebel, Fletcher and Gerald S. Clay. *Before You Sue: How to Get Justice Without Going to Court* (New York, William Morrow, 1987).

Kolb, Deborah M. (Ed.). *When Talk Works* (San Francisco, Jossey-Bass, 1994).

Kouzes, James and Barry Posner. *Credibility* (San Francisco, Jossey-Bass, 1993).

Kouzes, James M. and Barry Z. Posner. *The Leadership Challenge* (San Francisco, Jossey-Bass, 1987).

La Chapelle, David. *Navigating the Tides of Change* (Gabriola Island, BC, New Society, 2001).

Levine, Stewart. *The Book of Agreement* (San Francisco, Berrett-Koehler, 2003).

Levy, Mark. *Accidental Genius* (San Francisco, Berrett-Koehler, 2000).

Llewellen, Karl. *The Bramble Bush* ((New York, Oceana, 1930).

Maltz, Maxwell, MD. *Psycho-Cybernetics* (New York, Simon & Schuster, 1960).

Marks, Susan Collin. *Watching the Wind* (Washington, U.S. Institute of Peace, 2000).

Maturana, Humberto. *The Tree of Knowledge* (Boston, Shambhala, 1992).

Mayer, Bernard. *The Dynamics of Conflict Resolution* (San Francisco, Jossey-Bass, 2000).

Mindell, Arnold. *The Leader as Martial Artist* (San Francisco, HarperCollins, 1992).

Moore, Thomas. *Care of the Soul* (New York, HarperCollins, 1992).

Morgen, Sharon Drew. *Selling with Integrity* (San Francisco, Berrett-Koehler, 1997).

Moss, Richard. *The Black Butterfly: An Invitation to Radical Aliveness* (Berkeley, Celestial Arts, 1986).

Moss, Richard. *The I That Is We* (Berkeley, Celestial Arts, 1981).

Naisbitt, John. *Megatrends* (New York, Warner, 1982).

Naisbitt, John and Patricia Aburdine. *Megatrends 2000* (New York, William Morrow, 1990).

Noll, Douglas. *Peacemaking* (Telford, PA, Cascadia, 2003).

Notarius, Clifford. *We Can Work It Out* (New York, Putnam, 1993).

Patterson, Kerry and Joseph Grenny, Ron McMillan, Al Switzler. *Crucial Confrontations* (New York, McGraw-Hill, 2005).

Patterson, Kerry and Joseph Grenny, Ron McMillan, Al Switzler. *Crucial Conversations* (New York, McGraw-Hill, 2002).

Peck, M. Scott. *The Road Less Traveled* (New York, Simon & Schuster, 1978).

Peters, Thomas J. *Thriving on Chaos* (New York, Alfred A. Knopf, 1987).

Peters, Thomas J. and Robert H. Waterman, Jr. *In Search of Excellence* (New York, Harper & Row, 1982).

Peters, Tom. *Liberation Management: Necessary Disorganization for the Nanosecond Nineties* (New York, Ballantine, 1992).

Price Waterhouse LLP. *The Paradox Principles* (Chicago 1996).

Quinn, Daniel. *Ishmael* (New York, Bantam/Turner, 1993).

Rand, Ayn. *Atlas Shrugged* (New York, Random House, 1957).

Rand, Ayn. *The Fountainhead* (New York, Bobbs-Merrill, 1943).

Reid, Alan. *Seeing Law Differently: Views from a Spiritual Path* (Ontario, Canada, Borderland, 1992).

Reina, Dennis S. and Michelle L. Reina. *Trust and Betrayal in the Workplace* (San Francisco, Berrett-Koehler, 1998, 2006).

Remen, Rachel Naomi, MD. *Kitchen Table Wisdom* (New York, Riverhead Books, 1996).

Ridley, Matt. *The Origins of Virtue* (New York, Viking-Penguin, 1997).

Robbins, Anthony. *Unlimited Power* (New York, Fawcett Columbine, 1986).

Rogers, Carl. *On Becoming a Person: A Therapist's View of Psychotherapy* (Boston, Houghton Mifflin, 1961).

Ruiz, Don Miguel. *The Four Agreements* (San Rafael, CA, Amber-Allen 1997).

Saint-Exupéry, Antoine de. *The Little Prince* (New York, Harcourt Brace Jovanovich, 1941).

Schmidt, Warren H. and B. J. Hately. *Is It Always Right to Be Right?* (New York, Amacom, 2001).

Scott, Gini Graham. *Work with Me* (Mountain View, CA, Davies Black, 2000).

Senge, Peter. *The Fifth Discipline* (New York, Currency/Doubleday, 1990).

Simmons, Annette. *Territorial Games* (New York, AMACOM, 1998).

Simmons, Annette. *The Story Factor* (Cambridge, MA, Perseus, 2001).

Stack, Jack. *The Great Game of Business* (New York, Doubleday, 1992).

Stoltz, Paul G. *Adversity Quotient @Work* (New York, Morrow, 2000).

Tapscott, Don and Anthony Williams. *Wikinomics* (New York, Penguin, 2006).

Toffler, Alvin. *Powershift: Knowledge, Wealth and Violence at the Edge of the 21st Century* (New York, Bantam, 1990).

Tolle, Eckart. *The Power of Now* (Novato, CA, New World Library, 2004).

Ury, William. *Getting Past No* (New York, Bantam, 1991).

Vail, Peter B. *Learning as a Way of Being* (San Francisco, Jossey-Bass, 1996).

Weaver, Richard and John Farrell. *Managers as Facilitators* (San Francisco, Berrett-Koehler, 1999).

Weeks, Dudley. *The Eight Essential Steps to Conflict Resolution* (New York, Putnam, 1994).

Weisbord, Marvin R. (Ed.). *Discovering Common Ground* (San Francisco, Berrett-Koehler, 1992).

Weisbord, Marvin R. and Sandra Janoff. *Future Search: An Action Guide to Finding Common Ground in Organizations and Communities* (San Francisco, Berrett-Koehler, 1995).

Weiss, Alan. *Life Balance* (San Francisco, Jossey-Bass, 2003).

Wheatley, Margaret. *Leadership and the New Science* (San Francisco, Berrett-Koehler, 1992).

Wheatley, Margaret and Myron Kellner Rogers. *A Simpler Way* (San Francisco, Berrett-Koehler, 1996).

Whyte, David. *The Heart Aroused* (New York, Currency Doubleday, 1996).

Wilbur, Ken. *A Brief History of Everything* (Boston, Shambhala, 2001).

Williams, Margery. *The Velveteen Rabbit or How Toys Become Real* (New York, Doubleday, 1922).

Wilson, Larry. *Changing the Game: The New Way to Sell* (New York, Fireside, 1987).

Wylie, Peter. *Can This Partnership Be Saved?* (Denver, Upstart Publishing, 1993).

Zaiss, Carl. *True Partnership* (San Francisco, Berrett-Koehler, 2002).

Zambucka, Kristin. *The Keepers of Earth* (Honolulu, Harrane, 1984).

Zambucka, Kristin. *The Mana Keepers* (Honolulu, Green Glass, 1990).

# Index

Chopra, Deepak, power to create
matter, 173
civility, adopting a mood of, 114
clarity, listening for, 98–99
Clydesdale horses, Budweiser wagon,
187
collaboration
articulating a joint vision, 181
creating synergy, 162
mindset of, 62
team formation, 56–57
common ground, listening for, 111
communications
becoming culturally multi-lingual,
130
democracy, xxii
enabling good, 128–129
establishing a dialogue between both
parties, 113–114
f2f (face to face) vs. virtual-world,
129–130
*See also* communications
competency, evaluating a
resolutionary's, 213–215
completion process
experiencing a cleansing expression,
146–147
getting all the details out in the
open, 42
letting go of the past and moving
toward the future, 145
purposes of, 143–145
concerns, addressing, 157, 165, 179
conditioning, adversarial, 78
conflict
agreements in lieu of, 167–168
choices for resolving, 204–205
costs of, 16–24
preveniton, 55
putting in the past, 168
resolving an intrapersonal, 196–197
spit happens, 60–61
unresolved, 5
congruity, checking for, 99
continuum, choices for dispute
resolution, 204–205
conversations
collaborative, 6–7
real-time, 152
serious, 192
cooperation, fostering an attitude of,
118–119

cost
emotional, 23
litigation, 12–13, 24
lost productivity, 19–20
opportunity, 20–21
replacing a fired employee, 23
court systems, traditional, 14
covenant
absence of, 88
agreements based upon, 6–7, 161
Covey, Stephen, *The Speed of Trust*, 95
Covey, Steven R.
empowering employees, 189
listening for the truth, 41
creativity
abundance, 48
disagreements, 67
improving, 190
promoting, 179–180
solutions based on issues, 218
wealth, 49
customers, satisfaction, 190

Darwin, Charles, the value of life, 53
Dawson, Roger, "power negotiating", 42
deadlines, time limits for, 165
deathbed, viewing end result from
your, 159
DeBono, Edward, secrecy and mistrust,
91
declarations, completion process, 150,
151
delegation, problem solving, 10
DePree, Max, covenantal relationships,
161
design, creative, 204
development, emotional, 63
dialogue
conflict resolution, 3
democracy, xxii
effective agreements, 39
keeping an open, 98
productive, 48
differences, dealing with, 177–178
disclosure
full, 94–95, 144, 181–182
rescuing a highway project by
promoting full, 94–95
disputes, the business of law, 205–206
Disraeli, being little, 224
diversity, issues of, 190–191
divorce, co-parenting after, 168

# About the Author

## Stewart Levine Is a "Resolutionary"

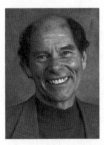

Stewart Levine is the founder of RESOLU-TIONWORKS. His personal mission is to promote collaboration and change the way our culture currently resolves conflicts: To become reliant on resolution and agreement for its business and personal relationships. *Getting to Resolution* is drawn from 35 years of experience as a lawyer, manager, consultant, mediator, and trainer.

He began his career advising and representing public officials as a deputy attorney general for the state of New Jersey. He practiced law actively for ten years, representing individuals and corporations in civil and criminal trials and overseeing complex commercial and real estate transactions. While working on his Master of Laws degree, he taught at Temple University Law School, where he was a law and humanities fellow.

In six years at AT&T, Levine was recognized as a pioneer "intrapreneur." He taught empowerment and intrapreneurial business development seminars to managers as the company moved through divestiture. He was a partner in charge of business development for a consulting company that moved from servicing the small business market to working with Fortune 500 companies.

Stewart combines a dynamic blend of powerful insight and creativity. He is a creative problem solver widely recognized for creating agreement and empowerment in the most challenging circumstances. He improves productivity while saving the enormous cost of conflict. His innovative work with Agreements for Results and his Resolutionary conversational models are unique. As a practicing lawyer, he realized that fighting was a very ineffective way of resolving problems. As a marketing executive for AT&T, he saw that the reason collaborations fall apart is that people do not spend the time at the beginning of new working relationships to create clarity about what they want to accomplish together and how they will get there. This is true for employment relationships, teams, joint ventures, and all members of any virtual team. As a result of his observations, he designed conversational models that create Agreements for Results, and a quick return to productivity when those working relationships break down. He uses his approach to form teams and joint ventures in a variety of situations. He works with individuals, couples, partners, and small and large organizations of all kinds.

Levine was a panelist for the San Francisco Bar Association Symposium on the Future of the Legal Profession. He held human resources appointments from the Law Practice Management Section of the American Bar Association. He has written a number of articles advocating resolution as the highest art of legal service. The ideas in Levine's articles were endorsed by the House Judiciary Committee in its examination of case resolution in the federal courts. These ideas appear as part of the *Congressional Record.*

His "Cycle of Resolution" was recently selected for inclusion in the *Change Handbook*, 2nd ed. The first edition of *Getting to Resolution* (Berrett-Koehler, 1998) was an Executive Book Club Selection; was featured by Executive Book Summaries; and named one of the 30 Best Business Books of 1998. It has been translated into Russian, Hebrew, and Portuguese. *The Book of Agreement* (Berrett-Koehler, 2003) has been endorsed by many thought leaders. It has been hailed as "more practical" than the classic *Getting to Yes*, and named one of the best books of 2003 by *CEO Refresher* (www.refresher.com). *Collaboration 2.0: Technology and Tools for Collaboration in a Web 2.0 World* co-authored with David Coleman (Happy About, 2008) provides guidance for communicating effectively in the virtual world.

Levine has trained companies in the United States, Australia, Canada, England, New Zealand, Ireland, Scotland, Colombia, and Mexico. He teaches programs on leadership, management, collaboration, communication, conflict resolution, and virtual communication. He has spoken before a broad range of audiences including American Bar Association; Association of Association Executives; Association of Legal Administrators; Association of Quality Participation; American Express; Canada Attorney General; Caterpillar Corporation; Chevron; ConAgra; Commonwealth Club of San Francisco; Deloitte & Touche; Genentech; EDS; Esalen Institute; General Motors; Harvard Law School; Herman Miller Corp.; Human Resource Planning Society; NVIDIA; Oracle; *Phil Donahue Show;* PMI; Safeco Insurance Company; U.S. Department of Agriculture; U.S. Army; EPA; NASA; Simon Fraser University Center for Management Innovation; Society for Human Resource

Managers; Society for Professionals In Dispute Resolution; Syracuse University Entrepreneurial Forum; University of Massachusetts; University of San Francisco; the U. S. Attorney's office; and Visa USA.

Stewart currently consults for The American Management Association, IBI Global, and the International Partnering Institute.

Stewart graduated from the Maxwell School of Economics at Syracuse University. He is an honors graduate of Rutgers Law School where he was Student Writing Editor of the *Law Review*. He lives and works in the San Francisco Bay Area.

# RESOLUTIONWORKS

Stewart Levine is the founder of ResolutionWorks. He is a coach, facilitator, mediator, and organizational educator. The mission of ResolutionWorks is creating cultures of Agreement and Resolution in organizations, government agencies, communities, and families. The content of this book and the programs he offers come from the lessons learned from the day-to-day practice of this work. If you are engaged and inspired by what you have experienced in this book, there is more on the path to becoming a "Resolutionary," a designation coined by an enthusiastic client with a flair for marketing. Most of our offerings are customized. We look forward to serving you in the following ways:

KEYNOTES — inspirational and content-rich

INTERVENTIONS — conflict, breakdowns, and challenging situations of all kinds

AGREEMENT/COLLABORATION — preventing conflict and generating high performance for start-ups, organizations, boards, executive teams, new teams, and new personal relationships

ORGANIZATIONS — building cultures of sustainable collaboration; retreat design and facilitation; aligning mission, vision, values and actions; communication skills; management development; creativity and innovation; building learning organizations; team formation and development

PERSONAL COACHING — custom-designed programs that maximize desired results and effectiveness

WORKSHOPS AND COURSES — long and short custom-designed offerings

PRODUCTS — books, e-books, audios, videos, and other digital programs and products

eLEARNING — proprietary offering available for groups or individuals

www.ResolutionWorks.com
email: ResolutionWorks@msn.com
skype: Stewart.Levine
land line (510) 777-1166    cell (510) 814-1010

# About Berrett-Koehler Publishers

Berrett-Koehler is an independent publisher dedicated to an ambitious mission: Creating a World That Works for All.

We believe that to truly create a better world, action is needed at all levels—individual, organizational, and societal. At the individual level, our publications help people align their lives with their values and with their aspirations for a better world. At the organizational level, our publications promote progressive leadership and management practices, socially responsible approaches to business, and humane and effective organizations. At the societal level, our publications advance social and economic justice, shared prosperity, sustainability, and new solutions to national and global issues.

A major theme of our publications is "Opening Up New Space." They challenge conventional thinking, introduce new ideas, and foster positive change. Their common quest is changing the underlying beliefs, mindsets, institutions, and structures that keep generating the same cycles of problems, no matter who our leaders are or what improvement programs we adopt.

We strive to practice what we preach—to operate our publishing company in line with the ideas in our books. At the core of our approach is *stewardship*, which we define as a deep sense of responsibility to administer the company for the benefit of all of our "stakeholder" groups: authors, customers, employees, investors, service providers, and the communities and environment around us.

We are grateful to the thousands of readers, authors, and other friends of the company who consider themselves to be part of the "BK Community." We hope that you, too, will join us in our mission.

# Be Connected

*Visit Our Website*

Go to www.bkconnection.com to read exclusive previews and excerpts of new books, find detailed information on all Berrett-Koehler titles and authors, browse subject-area libraries of books, and get special discounts.

*Subscribe to Our Free E-Newsletter*

Be the first to hear about new publications, special discount offers, exclusive articles, news about bestsellers, and more! Get on the list for our free e-newsletter by going to www.bkconnection.com.

*Get Quantity Discounts*

Berrett-Koehler books are available at quantity discounts for orders of ten or more copies. Please call us toll-free at (800) 929-2929 or email us at bkp.orders@aidcvt.com.

*Host a Reading Group*

For tips on how to form and carry on a book reading group in your workplace or community, see our website at www.bkconnection.com.

*Join the BK Community*

Thousands of readers of our books have become part of the "BK Community" by participating in events featuring our authors, reviewing draft manuscripts of forthcoming books, spreading the word about their favorite books, and supporting our publishing program in other ways. If you would like to join the BK Community, please contact us at bkcommunity@bkpub.com.